In the Eye of the Wind

**OPERATION
DRAKE**

In the
Eye of the Wind

The Story of Operation Drake

Roger Chapman

Hamish Hamilton *London*

Acknowledgments

Operation Drake was one of the largest and most complex expeditions ever to leave Britain. It is impossible to mention by name all the thousands of sponsors, administrators, scientists and servicemen who made it possible, or the young explorers who gave it its unique vitality.

However, I would like to thank the twelve young explorers who kindly told me of their experiences on the expedition and whose stories are related in this book. I would also like to thank Christopher Sainsbury, the expedition photographer, who checked all the facts and helped select the photographs; Andrew Mitchell, the scientific co-ordinator, for reading proofs; Christine Sandeman, who so expertly edited the book and saw it through its various traumas; and, finally, John Blashford-Snell, Chairman of the Scientific Exploration Society, whose leadership, inspiration and drive gave the opportunity to so many to spend part of their lives in the *Eye of the Wind*.

Photographs: I would like to thank Christopher Sainsbury, Borkur Arnvidarson, Hamish Brown, Richard Davis, Desmond Dugan, Rupert Grey, the Kenya Wildlife Conservation and Management Department, Nigel Lang, Rupert Ridgeway, Richard Sailer and Ian Swingland for permission to use their photographs.

Book design by Tim Higgins
Jacket design by Don Macpherson
Maps by Tony Garrett

First published in Great Britain 1982 by
Hamish Hamilton Children's Books
Garden House, 57–59 Long Acre, London WC2E 9JZ
Copyright © 1982 by The Scientific Exploration Society
and Roger Chapman
All rights reserved.

British Library Cataloguing in Publication Data
In the eye of the wind
1 Operation Drake, (1978-1980)
I. Title
910.4 G419.D/
ISBN 0 241 10764 4

Printed in Great Britain by
Thomson Litho Ltd, East Kilbride, Scotland

Contents

Foreword

HRH The Prince of Wales
Patron of Operation Drake

As Patron, I watched the progress of Operation Drake with interest. I think that we can all feel well satisfied that the expedition has been an outstanding success. I have been particularly pleased to see how the Young Explorers have been able to make a genuine contribution to the many scientific projects. I hope this can be an example to others of how simple scientific studies can be completed by young people, even though at the outset they may have been lacking in any specialist knowledge. Much of the expedition's programme has been concerned with conservation studies. I am hopeful that in due course the results will make a modest contribution towards encouraging the conservation of our natural resources.

Operation Drake has provided opportunities for a great many Young Explorers to work and live amongst people of other countries and contribute towards a better understanding of one another. Often projects have been conducted in remote areas and under arduous conditions, which have provided both adventure and an opportunity for the Young Explorers to stretch themselves mentally and physically. If, as I hope will be the case, the young people who write of their experiences in *In the Eye of the Wind* transmit their enthusiasm to others to seek to put their skills in service to the community – then the aims of Operation Drake and this book will truly have been fulfilled.

Charles.

Introduction

Roger Chapman

In late November 1980, a square-rigged* sailing ship approached Plymouth Sound. The 150-tonne brigantine* *Eye of the Wind* was returning to England after battling for two years across the world's oceans, anchoring off every kind of shore, and taking part in dozens of projects. Now this adventure was at an end; the circumnavigation of the world was complete.

The young crew of the *Eye of the Wind* had little sleep during that final leg of the voyage to England. For two days, during a terrible storm, most had been on deck or aloft*, changing or furling* sails. They hadn't even had time to get out of their sweaters and oilskins. One young girl from Plymouth scanned the familiar coastline from the foredeck*. As the brigantine lifted on the next huge wave, she pointed to some low-lying rocks at the mouth of the river leading to Plymouth harbour. She had to shout to be heard above the roar of the sea and scream of the gulls. 'There it is . . . Drake's Island.'

The island – like the expedition – had been named after Francis Drake, one of the greatest sailors ever born. At that exact spot, 400 years before, another sailing ship had waited for the tide. Like the *Eye of the Wind*, the *Golden Hind* had circumnavigated the world. It had taken Francis Drake and his crew of fifty-seven sailors three years. Between 1577 and 1580 they had faced storms, shipwreck, mutiny and disease; they had plundered Spanish settlements on the west coast of the Americas; they had fought pitched battles and landed on unknown shores. Then they had returned to England with treasures beyond their wildest dreams. The hold* of their sturdy galleon* was crammed with stacks of silver bars, gold coins and piles of precious emeralds, diamonds and pearls. As the wind and waves inched the *Golden Hind* towards the line of rocks which jut up at the head of the estuary, Francis

*Explanations of starred words can be found in the Glossary on p.127.

Opposite
Over 250 Young Explorers (aged 17–24 years) from 27 different countries experienced 'life before the mast' during the sea phases of this two year expedition.

Drake saw two fishing boats bobbing close to the island's rocky shore. He leaned over the handrail of the poop deck* and bellowed, 'Does the Queen live?'

The fishermen continued to pull in their nets as if unaware of the approach of the 120-tonne galleon. Then one old man slowly looked up. 'Aye, the Queen lives.' A ragged cheer rose from the crew of the *Golden Hind*, for they now knew that they could return to England in safety and triumph. Had Queen Elizabeth I been succeeded by a monarch friendly to Spain, there would have been little chance of Drake and his men escaping with their lives. When Queen Elizabeth heard of the safe return of the *Golden Hind* she ordered Francis Drake to sail up the Thames to London.

When Drake reached Deptford in April 1581, he gave orders for the finest jewels to be picked out and laid on the captain's table as a gift for Her Majesty the Queen. In all, over half a million pounds of silver and gold had been plundered from the Spanish, more than enough to fill England's empty coffers. After dining on board, the Queen and her courtiers went out on the red-carpeted quarterdeck* of the freshly painted galleon. She asked the French Ambassador to take his sword and lightly touch the kneeling Drake on the shoulder, 'Arise, *Sir* Francis Drake.' His knighthood was a fitting end to an epic voyage and a great adventure. It was a supreme honour for the first English sea captain to circumnavigate the world.

Operation Drake – a mammoth expedition for young people from many countries – had been planned to give these young people a chance to re-awaken and commemorate that old Elizabethan spirit of challenge and adventure. On his return to England the skipper of the *Eye of the Wind*, like his illustrious predecessor, was asked to take his ship up the Thames to London. On 13 December 1980, with the young members of his crew manning the yardarms*, the white-painted brigantine motored slowly past the grey columns of Greenwich Naval College towards the Tower of London.

The air was filled with the hoots of tug horns, martial music from military bands on the quay, and the cheers of thousands of well-wishers, who lined both banks to see the flagship of Operation Drake arrive in the heart of London. Slowly Tower Bridge parted to allow the tall masts of the brigantine through. At that moment a jaunty Beaver spotter-plane flew low over the bridge, followed by a mammoth Hercules transport aircraft, similar to those that had carried stores and supplies to the expedition in all parts of the world.

In the crowd were many of those 2,000 administrators, servicemen, sponsors, scientists and Young Explorers who had helped make possible one of the great adventures of modern times. Over 200 of the 414 Young Explorers from twenty-seven different countries had travelled to London for the homecoming celebrations. They were aged between seventeen and twenty-four and had been selected from over 58,000 applicants to represent their countries on one of the nine phases of Operation Drake.

During the past two years, each of those Young Explorers had spent three months both on board the *Eye of the Wind* and on one of the land-based expeditions in Panama, Papua New Guinea, Indonesia and East Africa. Often their experiences had been unpleasant, frightening or uncomfortable. But they carried on to conduct projects in remote parts of the world very different from their own. They had worked with scientists on wildlife conservation studies, excavated ancient cities, carried out community projects and conducted research surveys amongst primitive peoples. In difficult conditions, they had stretched themselves physically and mentally to complete their work. In doing so, they had displayed the same determination and spirit that Sir Francis Drake and his crew had shown 400 years before. Now they too had a story to tell.

The *Golden Hind*

Galleon
Circumnavigation
1577–1580

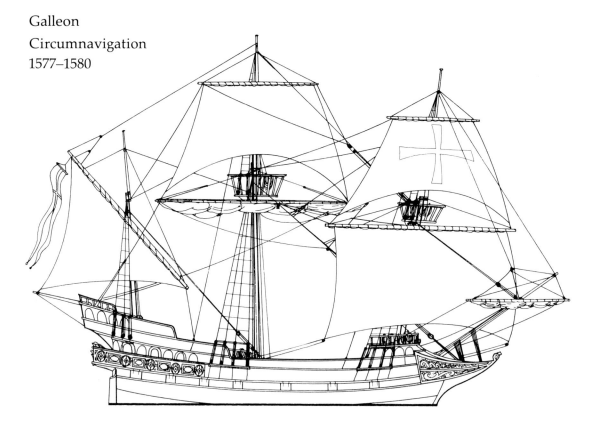

The *Golden Hind* was built as an armed warship, with seven gun ports on each side, two guns to the stern and two in the bows – eighteen cannons in all.

Francis Drake slept in a comfortable cabin and employed musicians to entertain him with music. His crew did not live so well. They had to survive on salt meat, fish, cheese and ships biscuits washed down with watery beer. Because they ate no fresh vegetables, many of them developed scurvy and died.

After the circumnavigation, the *Golden Hind* was berthed at Deptford, where it attracted many visitors. But in about 1662, after eighty years of neglect, the ship broke up on the mud banks and vanished without trace.

Length	32 metres overall
	30 metres waterline
Beam	7 metres
Weight	120 tonnes gross
Crew	10 officers and 80 sailors and marines
Accommodation	The officers slept in bunks in a cabin measuring 5 metres × 8 metres. The crew slept below in former storage holds

Navigation Techniques	Quadrant, astrolabe and cross staff
	Compass and log
	Simple charts and dead reckoning
Rig	2 masts and 5 square sails
Speed	average 3–5 knots
	maximum 7 knots
Armament	18 cannons

The *Eye of the Wind*

Brigantine
Circumnavigation
1978–1980

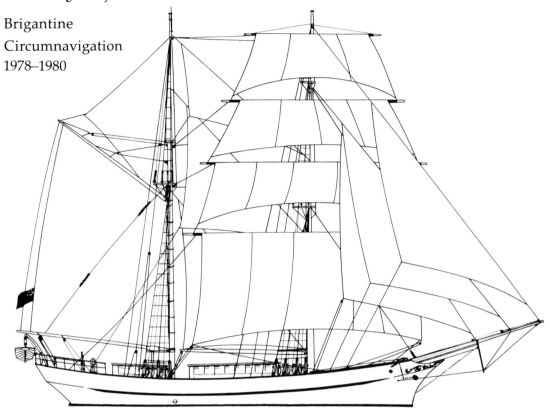

The *Eye of the Wind* was built in 1911 near Bremen in West Germany. For many years, she was used on a variety of trade routes. But in 1969 she was gutted by fire, and it was not until 1973 that she was bought by her present owners, the Adventure Under Sail syndicate. In 1976 she was completely restored for world-wide cruising.

A scientific laboratory was constructed and fully equipped and the cabins were altered to make them suitable for the voyage. A well-equipped galley ensured that the Young Explorers had three good meals a day cooked on gas stoves. There was also a fridge, deep freezer and comfortable saloon, fitted with a well-stocked library and games, for the Young Explorers to relax in during the long voyage.

Length	41 metres overall
	30 metres waterline
Beam	7 metres
Weight	150 tonnes gross
Crew	36 male and female
Accommodation	12 cabins with 2 or 4 people to a cabin (2 × 3 metres), 1 galley, 1 saloon, 1 chart room, 1 radio room, 1 engine room

Navigation Techniques	Sextant, marine radio, compass, modern charts, depth finder
Rig	2 masts and 15 sails (6 of which are square sails)
Speed	average 6–8 knots maximum 10–15 knots
Engine	220 h.p. Gardiner engine

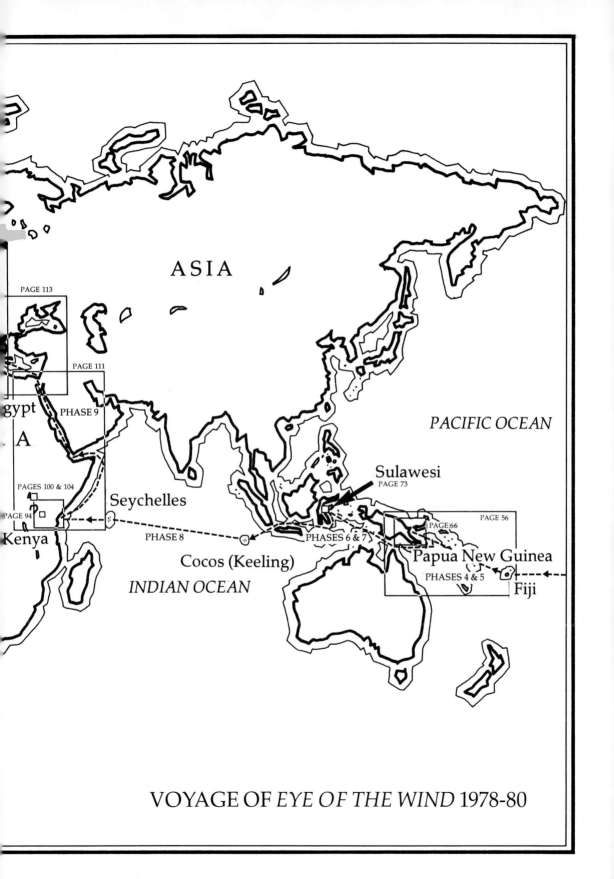

ASIA

PAGE 113

PAGE 111

gypt

PHASE 9

A

PACIFIC OCEAN

PAGES 100 & 104

Seychelles

Sulawesi
PAGE 73

PAGE 94

PAGE 56

PAGE 66

Kenya

PHASE 8

PHASES 6 & 7

Cocos (Keeling)

Papua New Guinea

INDIAN OCEAN

PHASES 4 & 5

Fiji

VOYAGE OF *EYE OF THE WIND* 1978-80

When Opportunity Knocks

Winston Bygrave *England*

I was hungry,
rather sleepy, and
a little bewildered,
but ready for
anything the
Operation Drake
selection team
set me – or
so I thought!

Winston Bygrave, a young civil servant living in London, was among thirty-three applicants to be chosen for one of the final selection weekends. He had heard about Operation Drake on the radio and read about it in the newspapers. He didn't think he had much of a chance of getting on it but decided to give it a try anyway. He filled in the three-page application form and posted it to the Headquarters of Operations in Whitehall.

A month later, he sat with a group of young people in a waiting-room outside an interview room. As he looked at the other applicants his heart sank. They all looked so much fitter, more confident, and more self-assured. 'Oh well,' he thought, 'I might as well give it a go.' At last, he was called in to face a panel of explorers, scientists and youth leaders, all seated behind a long table.

'What can you contribute to Operation Drake?' 'What qualities do you think you will have to have on an expedition?' 'What

Opposite
Abseiling down a sheer rock face was one of the many tests set by Operation Drake's selection teams to choose future Young Explorers.

do you consider your participation on Operation Drake will do to help the others?' Over the next half hour, the questions came thick and fast.

Elsewhere, in other parts of Britain, in Australia, Canada, New Zealand, and the United States, other young hopefuls were facing similar interviews. Committees there, and in many other countries around the world, had been formed over the previous six months to choose people from their own country to join Operation Drake. They had been set up under the guidance of Lieutenant-Colonel John Blashford-Snell, who had first thought up the idea of a round-the-world expedition for young people four years before.

But how did they make a fair choice from so many applicants? It could only be done by a searching interview and a very tough selection weekend; testing competence in living in the field, compatibility, unselfishness, and adaptability under adverse conditions. It was important, too, to find out if the applicant had a sense of humour.

After I'd been told I'd passed my interview, I got a letter telling me to report one Saturday morning to a small village in the mountainous area of mid-Wales. I was given a grid reference for the small village of Pennal and told to be there at 10.30 a.m. on 28 October 1978. I was to take enough equipment to last or, should I say, endure two nights in the mountains.

When I arrived the judges took our names and gave us each a number to tie on. I was number 20. 'At least there's one thing to be thankful for', I thought. 'It could have been number 13!' We were then given the grid reference for an abandoned slate-mine near a dried-up reservoir. On my map it looked about 7 kilometres away. We were told to find our way there, and when we'd arrived to check it out and write a report about it. Everything went without a hitch, except when I had to walk through a herd of cows. I thought I might be chased by a bull. I was wearing a bright red windcheater! Luckily, they didn't take any notice of me.

After we'd written our reports we were split into groups of five. Each group was given a stretcher and told to tie their rucksacks onto it. Then one of the judges said, 'Imagine you're deep in a tropical rain forest. One of your party has fallen critically ill, and you have to take him back to your base camp for medical care. Speed is essential.' (Imagine was a word the judges were to use again and again that weekend.) The quickest route, in our case, was to follow a

river which was cascading down a gully. It led to the village many thousands of metres below. I thought to myself, 'What does he mean – "take the quickest route down to the river?" He can't mean we're going to walk in the river, can he?' Just before the different teams left, another judge advised us to keep our sense of humour. 'That won't be difficult,' I thought. 'I'm always cheerful.' Little did I realise how difficult it would be to follow his advice.

We set off down some of the most difficult country I've ever travelled. It was made more difficult by the fact that we had to carry the laden stretcher. Then one of the girls in our group sprained her ankle. Sense of humour indeed! 'Keep it moving', the judges cried, 'remember, for *that* person on the stretcher, it's a matter of life and death.'

After fifteen minutes of slipping, slithering, grunting and groaning, we were exhausted. I began to see these judges as mad sadists. Then I heard something I hoped I hadn't heard. 'Get into the river!' Suddenly I realised why the judge was wearing wet-suit trousers. It wouldn't have been so bad if the water had been ankle-deep, but the judge sank up to his waist in water. I began to realise that these people meant business; it wasn't going to be the glorified camping weekend I had thought.

Selection weekends took place in many countries around the world. There were over 58,000 applications for 414 places.

Right Jenny Warne and Winston Bygrave, seen here making an improvised stretcher, were two of the English candidates who were finally selected to go on Operation Drake.

Below One test on selection weekends was to weigh a 4-metre-long python. This one, nicknamed 'Monty Python', weighed over 18 kilogrammes.

At first I didn't want to get in the water. But when one of the girls jumped in, I thought 'If she can do it, so can I.' The water was FREEZING. We struggled down that river for what seemed like ages, slipping on wet rocks and moss-covered stones, just keeping the stretcher and our rucksacks out of the water. Finally we arrived, totally exhausted.

A van took us to the Adventure Centre at Celmi which was to be our base for the weekend. It was an old farmhouse with many outhouses and barns on the side of a windswept mountain. Again, we were divided into teams and told to cook our meal for the day and build a shelter for the night. The food consisted of frozen mackerel, raw potatoes, carrots and onions. While some of us struggled to get the fire going in the drizzling rain, others tried to construct a shelter out of plastic sheeting. The rest of the group was taken off for further tests. Since I was cooking, I was the last to go.

To start with, I had to fire a shotgun. It was the first time in my life. Fantastic! I think I missed, but it was good fun all the same. Then I was taken into a dark room. On a table there were some bowls with various objects inside which I had to recognise by touch. This wasn't difficult, even though my hands were frozen.

The final test took me completely by surprise. I was taken into a shed where I could see two sheep huddled in a corner. I was asked to weigh one with a set of bathroom scales. 'Ha ha, very clever,' I thought. 'You can't fool me.' All I needed to do was weigh myself, pick one up and stand on the scales. A quick subtraction would give me the weight of the sheep. Easy!

But first I had to catch the sheep. I chased them round and round the shed. They were scared of me, almost as scared as I was of them. I paused for breath and started again. This was getting embarrassing. At last I cornered one and caught it. The surprising thing was that once I'd got hold of it, the sheep became abolutely still, making it very easy to pick up and weigh. I heard later that some people tried to sit the sheep on the bathroom scales and then read its weight!

I went back to our camp site. I was so hungry that I didn't mind eating half-raw fish and undercooked vegetables. In fact, it was one of the best meals I'd had for a long time.

In another test, we were to imagine – yes, that word again – that we were in a tropical rain forest without a torch or light. To make sure we couldn't see we had to put a rucksack over our heads. My heart began to beat faster, as I was led by the hand to the starting point. My hand was placed on the rope. Slowly I began to move. I had only gone 20 cautious metres when suddenly I felt my feet sink into slimy mud. 'That's it', I told myself, 'I'm going back. A joke's a joke, they're taking this too far.' Slowly I inched my way back, only to bump into the next candidate. I stopped and he carefully groped his way past me.

'Number 20, are you going to move or not?' I stood still and began to think. How tough I had always thought myself to be – and here I was ready to give in. Should I accept defeat or go on? While I stood there wondering what to do, I began to realise what the examiners were trying to do – assuming they weren't trying to kill me! They looked upon Operation Drake as a very serious test whereas, until that moment, I had looked on it as just another jolly. They were sorting out the men from the boys, the women from the girls. They weren't looking at how we behaved or survived in normal conditions but how we acted in *ab*normal conditions.

I decided to accept the challenge. From that moment on, I went all out to prove to myself that I was man enough to finish. I moved forward and though the mud sometimes reached above my knees, and my boots filled with water, I didn't care. All I did care about was conquering this and any other test they cared to put in my way. I couldn't see so I allowed my other senses to do some of my eyes' work and it soon became quite easy to move through the swamp. I even found that my sense of humour returned. Finally I got to the end and was greeted with praise. 'Well done, Number 20'.

Other tests we had to do included building a raft, rock-climbing and abseiling down a rock face. Finally, at the end of the weekend, we had to give a 3-minute talk. Originally I'd planned to give my talk on how I'd prepared myself for Operation Drake. But after this weekend I realised that I hadn't been prepared at all. Instead I decided to talk honestly, without notes, on 'How my views have changed during the selection weekend'. I didn't plan it to be funny, but talking about all the incredible things we'd been through made everyone laugh. All I was really trying to say was that I'd learned there was more to expeditions than meets the eye. Above all, you have to learn to work with other people in difficult situations if you're going to have any hope of success. Expeditions are really all about people. When I finished my talk, standing on a box in the barn at Celmi Adventure Centre, I was surprised to receive loud applause. I can only assume that the other candidates had learned the same lessons.

We ended the weekend with an enormous meal. We had all survived an ordeal and had lots to talk to each other about. Strangely, I found that I was sorry to leave. I had made many friends.

I didn't expect to be chosen. In fact I wouldn't have minded that much . . . I'd found out so much about myself in those two days. But on the following Tuesday, I received a telephone call from the chief judge. I'd been selected for a place on Operation Drake and would be sponsored for £2,000 to participate in one of the three-month phases. Could I please write back formally accepting the place and let HQ Op. Drake know which phase I would like to attend?

'Fantastic,' I shouted. 'Where's my pen and paper? I'm on my way . . .'

Winston Bygrave spent three months in the rain forests of Sulawesi in Indonesia helping to prepare a management plan for a proposed nature reserve. Since his return, he has devoted a great deal of his time to being a volunteer community worker in the inner city areas of London.

PHASE 1   November 1978 – January 1979

All Hands on Deck

Gudjon Arngrimsson *Iceland*

'Faller fararheill' is an old Icelandic saying which is often quoted by fishermen along our coast. A rough translation would be: 'Every trip that starts badly has a good end.' It's an apt description of my three months with Operation Drake.

Gudjon Arngrimsson was twenty-three years old when he heard that he'd been selected for Operation Drake. He came from Reykjavik, the capital of Iceland, and like many of his country-men, had some experience of the sea. But though he had worked with fishing fleets in the North Sea and around the bays and inlets of his own country, he had never sailed in a ship such as the brigantine Eye of the Wind, *which was to act as his home for three months on Phase 1 of Operation Drake.*

In August 1978, Gudjon joined twenty-three other Young Explorers, or YE's as they were called, and the permanent crew of the Eye of the Wind *at Plymouth on the south coast of England. The YE's were aged between seventeen and twenty-four and represented seven different countries from around the world. They had been selected from thousands of applicants who all wanted to join what HRH The Prince of Wales had called 'a chance of a lifetime with all the challenges of war in peacetime'. It was the first of nine three-month phases which would take young people across the Atlantic, Pacific and Indian Oceans to join four major land-based expeditions in Panama, Papua New Guinea, Sulawesi and Kenya, before returning to England at the end of 1980.*

We all thought that we'd be off in a few days. But this wasn't to be the case. The ship – God bless her – was far from ready. So, for over a month, the YE's and lots of other people worked to get her seaworthy. At first we were a bit disappointed by the delay. But later, as we got to know each other, we realised that it wasn't such a bad thing after all. It's amazing how quickly you can get to know other people when you're preparing for a long sea voyage. Together, we really enjoyed those usually boring and dreary jobs such as painting, scraping, chipping, sewing, washing and, of course, drinking cups of tea. For me, an Icelander, drinking tea is quite a job!

On 22 October, the ship was sparkling; we had finished polishing all the brass and painting the hull* a brilliant white. The *Eye of the Wind* was now ready for Prince Charles, our patron, to come down and say 'goodbye'. The day he came turned into one long party. The Prince gave a short speech, then came aboard and chatted with each of us. He asked me about Iceland and the Icelanders. He knows Iceland because he usually visits it once a year for salmon fishing. But there were still a lot of things to do to the ship, including fitting a new 220 h.p. engine. As a result, the actual voyage didn't start until two weeks later, on 7 November. Even then our troubles weren't quite over because on the night we were due to leave there was a terrible storm. The English Channel became far too choppy for us to set sail, and we had to wait in harbour until the wind died down. But at last we were off and, after a short stop in Jersey, one of the Channel Islands, we headed towards the Bay of Biscay. The expedition had begun.

The Bay of Biscay is one of the roughest stretches of ocean in the world. Waves can be over 10 metres high and storms can blow continuously for days on end. The Bay is an extension of the North Atlantic Ocean and is bounded to the east and north-east by France and to the south by Spain. Heavy seas are commonplace because of the Bay's open situation to the Atlantic coupled with the shallowness of the sea-bed; the deepest part of the Bay is only 5,000 metres. The continental shelf below the waves stretches out from the coast, about 150 kilometres wide off Brittany, but gradually narrowing to less than 60 kilometres near Spain. It is a dangerous stretch of water for sailing ships.

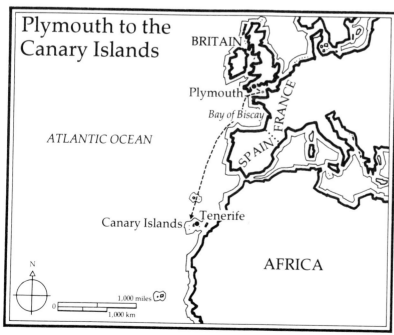

Plymouth to the Canary Islands

BRITAIN

Plymouth

Bay of Biscay

ATLANTIC OCEAN

SPAIN FRANCE

Canary Islands · Tenerife

AFRICA

N

0   1,000 miles
    1,000 km

The Eye of the Wind *passes Drake's Island as she leaves Plymouth. Operation Drake's patron, The Prince of Wales, is at the helm.*

Before long, several YE's became very seasick and had to stay in their bunks. This meant that the rest of us had more work to do. We worked in shifts; six of us on each watch. Each watch was on duty for four hours, rested for eight hours, then went on duty again. There were four watches altogether. The fourth watch spent the whole day in the galley*, cooking and washing. Cooking a meal in very heavy seas is very tricky. Have you ever tried to fry forty eggs on a rocking, swaying boat?! I bet you haven't.

But whatever the weather, we had to go up the rigging*. This meant holding on as tight as we could to a slippery rope, working our way carefully along the yardarms* and remembering *not* to look down. Below, the swaying ship looked very small and fragile amidst the green racing waves. The roaring wind almost blew us off. I've never been so scared in my life.

At last, after fifteen and a half days at sea, the weather settled down and we came in sight of Tenerife, in the Canary

Rory O'Connor (England), Sasha Campbell (Jersey) and the First Mate of the Eye of the Wind, *'Tiger' Timbs, hoist the main sail to catch the full power of the trade winds across the Atlantic Ocean.*

Islands. There are seven major islands and six smaller uninhabited islets in the Canaries. They are said to have got their
name because they were once full of dogs (or canines).
Living in a ship that's only 41 metres long with thirty-five
other people can get quite claustrophobic. The thought of
stepping onto dry land seemed too good to be true. It was
difficult to decide what to do first: whether to go for a walk –
something you can't do on board – or have a slap-up meal.

We had sailed south so that we could pick up the trade
winds which would blow us across the Atlantic Ocean.
Trade winds blow from east to west all the year round.
Sailing ships don't usually cross the Atlantic except in this
area just north of the Equator. Here the winds are steady and
safe and the weather perfect. There's sunshine all day long
with temperatures ranging between 20 and 30 degrees
Centigrade. Fortunately, there's always a refreshing breeze.
This part of the journey was very different from the voyage
down to Tenerife when the winds were gusty and often
violent and we had to work continually in the rigging.
During the next three weeks we hardly touched the sails*.
Bliss.

But we certainly weren't bored; there was always so much
to do. Our day began at 7 a.m. with an English-style
breakfast – porridge, eggs and bacon, toast, butter and mar-
malade and fruit. Everyone drank tea. In Iceland we usually
only have one cup of black coffee. On board at 8.30 a.m. we
had 'happy hour' – when we cleaned the ship. Because of the
watch system, this was the only time in the day we all
worked together. At 10.30 a.m. we had another cup of tea,
and at midday an enormous lunch. After lunch we had more
tea; we stopped for yet more tea at 3 p.m. and finally, after
our large evening meal at 5.30 p.m., we had our final cup of
tea. 'These British can never drink enough', I thought. After
dinner, we sat below in the saloon, drank a beer or soft
drink, played cards or games or just read, talked and
generally relaxed.

As we got closer to the warm Caribbean waters, we made
regular stops for a swim. The weather was now very hot and
we all needed frequent baths. Some YE's dived from the
rigging.

One day we were visited by a whale. It was first spotted
about 100 metres away from the ship, jumping clear out of
the water and landing with a great splash. About two hours
later we saw it under the the ship. It stayed there for the next
five days or so. Sometimes it swam in small circles behind

the ship, then out onto the starboard side, but most of the time it played happily with the hull. Maybe it thought that the ship was its mother.

During the crossing we were all given jobs to help with the marine biology programme. Mine was to fish, but unfortunately I only managed to get two or three on my hook. They were not very attractive fish or of much interest to Dr Trish Holdway, the marine biologist, but Lesley Reiter, our purser, managed to turn them into a good lunch. She could work miracles in that galley.

Other people examined the water for oil pollution, collected plankton, scraped barnacles off the hull and keel* to find out how and why they attached themselves to ships, and looked at food chains in the sea.

On 21 December we arrived in Bridgetown, Barbados, and from there it was only twelve hours' sailing to St Vincent, where we had a real job of work to do. We were to try and find out if the volcano, called La Soufrière, in the middle of the island was about to erupt again. The sides of the volcano rose to the lip of a crater which was over 2 kilometres in diameter. The steep edges of the crater plunged down 200 metres to a large lake which was over 1.5 kilometres in diameter and circled a small rock island. Since the volcano's last eruption in 1971 the temperature of the lake had dropped to about 25 degrees Centigrade. The only way to tell whether an eruption was due was to test whether the temperature of the lake dramatically rose and whether the water changed from a deep turquoise to a muddy mustard colour.

On 24 December we were woken at 4 a.m. to be taken by lorry to the foot of the mountain. Here we began the 1,000-metre ascent. Fortunately, it was cool in the early morning

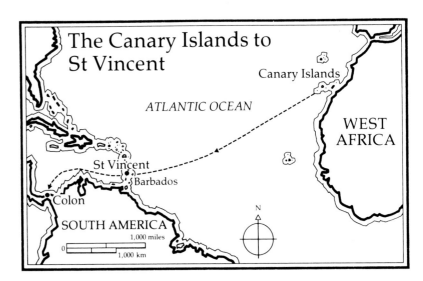

The Canary Islands to St Vincent

Canary Islands

ATLANTIC OCEAN

WEST AFRICA

St Vincent

Barbados

Colon

SOUTH AMERICA

1,000 miles

1,000 km

N

and as we got a little higher it became misty. It never got too hot. But the walk was difficult enough, even without the heat, because we were carrying heavy scientific equipment, a rubber inflatable dinghy and many ropes. We aimed to get down the 200-metres-deep crater, row our boat over the lake and see if there was any life on the island.

In the crater it was very hot and humid. It smelt too. The lake water was really hot, well over 30 degrees Centigrade, and the island was steaming and brown like a sleeping monster. We didn't have much time, because no-one wanted to be trapped down in the crater after dark, especially on Christmas Eve. So, after writing up all the results of the experiments conducted in the lake and on the island, we loaded our rucksacks, deflated the boat and started to scramble out of the crater. What a struggle we had to get the inflatable rubber boat up the 45-degree slope. It took eighteen of us, with one shouting commands! The trouble was that it was so rough underfoot. People kept slipping and

Gudjon Arngrimsson, in the white hat, shouts instructions as an Avon inflatable raft is lowered 300 metres down the inner crater of La Soufrière to the volcanic lake. La Soufrière erupted three months after this photo was taken.

In places, the water of the lake was so hot that the crew of the raft were worried that the tubes might burst. They were the last people to set foot on the volcanic island in the centre of the lake before the latest volcanic eruption.

sliding and falling down. If things had got out of control we could have had a nasty accident with everyone falling over and tumbling into the lake.

Eventually we emerged from the crater and started to slide down the side of the volcano as fast as we could. We found the lorry just before sunset. As we clambered into the back of the lorry, a tremendous tropical downpour hit us. How it rained! There we sat tired, soaking wet, cold and miserable. What a way to spend Christmas Eve.

Three months after the departure of the *Eye of the Wind*, as our findings were being studied in the University of the West Indies, La Soufrière erupted once more. It resulted in the evacuation of some 20,000 of the 96,000 islanders, although luckily no-one was killed. We were the last people to enter the crater before the eruption, and the last people to visit the island in the centre of the lake.

Next morning we set sail on the last part of our voyage across the Caribbean to Panama. Once the sails were set, we were able to settle down and enjoy Christmas. We had a large turkey for dinner plus a couple of bottles of champagne. There was also a small present for everyone on board bought from a kitty which we had contributed towards over the past month.

On 2 January we arrived in Colon, Panama, having set a new speed record of 323 kilometres in one day. In some parts of the city the houses and streets were old and elegant; but

the ghettos were squalid. The people were generally friendly but we'd been told that at night Colon was one of the most dangerous cities in the world. We soon found out how true this was. When we went into the city on our first evening, we split into four groups, with about eight in each group. We were all big, healthy and strong but even so two of the groups were attacked by street gangs. Steve, our engineer, was taken to hospital with a broken cheek bone and lots of bruises. For him the trip was over.

The next day we were flown from Panama City to Caledonia Bay on the north-east coast of the Darien Isthmus facing the Caribbean Sea. Caledonia Bay was the sheltered harbour where Sir Francis Drake used to hide from pirate ships and wait for Spanish plunder. In those days, he knew it as Pheasant Bay. In the seventeenth century it was the site of a Scottish colony. Now, in the twentieth century, it was to be the base for the first land phase of Operation Drake.

We landed on the half-completed airstrip at Caledonia Bay to discover that our first job was to chop down the vegetation at the far end of the runway. Everything at base camp was rather primitive: no huts or houses, just army tents; no electricity, just paraffin lamps; salty water and food out of tins. There was every type of insect you could think of. Some were so small that even mosquito nets couldn't keep them out. We were bitten to pieces by the wretched sandflies. I was always afraid of snakes. They could be lurking on any path in the jungle or lie curled under your camp bed at night. The bush master, South America's most poisonous snake, was sighted near the camp and the fer de lance, the world's fastest snake, could be found all over Darien. For the most part, the jungle and I didn't get along. It was unbearably hot and humid and every sandfly in South America must have had a nibble at me at some time or other. Even so, there were times when you couldn't help but be moved by its grandeur.

I got on with the sea a lot better than with the jungle. Diving down to the strangely-coloured coral beds was wonderful. There were hundreds of different sorts of coral; huge brain corals which look as though they'd been dragged from some dying giant's head, stag horn coral with its crazy twisted shapes and fan coral, bright purple and wafting in the light swells of Caledonia Bay.

The tasks were endless: we took turns at the cooking, cleaning and scrubbing; we cleared the site for the archaeological excavations and helped to sift the earth; we did a bit of diving in the Bay helping the marine archaeologists, and took supplies through the forest to the scientists who were working to finish building an aerial walkway. This was erected at a height of about 40 metres so that the scientists could study the jungle canopy.

Usually we were up before 6 a.m. to avoid the worst of the heat during our main hours of work but we had to take a siesta at midday because of the intense rays of the sun. We then worked with the scientists until the evening meal at 5 p.m. It got dark at 6 p.m. By that time, most of us were usually so tired that we collapsed exhausted into our hammocks. We fell asleep listening to the eerie sounds from the tropical rain forest around us.

By the time our phase came to an end in mid-January, we knew each other like brothers and sisters. Saying goodbye was very difficult. We all talked about visiting each other and meeting again, but most of us realised that this might well never happen. That's life I'm afraid. But, we'll never forget our times together. Happy days. Above all, I'll never forget the *Eye of the Wind* and those magic moments at sea under sail.

Gudjon Arngrimsson returned to Iceland to work on one of the country's leading national newspapers. His first major article was about his experiences crossing the Atlantic Ocean on Operation Drake.

PHASE 2   January 1979 – April 1979

Scots Awa'

Cathy Davies *Scotland*

As you enter the rain forest, you're amazed how dark and cool it is. Trees soar up into the green canopy of leaves above, like the columns of a medieval cathedral. It's rather strange and eerie at first. Sunbeams only break through where a tree, rotten with age, has crashed to the ground and left a gap in the canopy, or where the local Indians or settlers have chopped down the trees to make a clearing. In these clearings there is dense, tangled foliage. We saw a forest like this on the shores of Caledonia Bay in Panama.

The rain forests of Darien can be forbidding – not an ideal spot to spend three months of your life. But Cathy Davies, an athletic seventeen-year-old schoolgirl from Edinburgh, wasn't worried; she couldn't wait to get out there. She had learned about the Scots' settlement in history lessons: how, in 1698, 2,000 Scots had attempted to found a colony on the Isthmus of Central America to link the Pacific trade with that of the Atlantic; and how disease, famine and Spanish attacks had quickly overcome the Scots of 'Caledonia', as their colony was called.

But although there were many records about the hardships and problems facing those early Scottish colonists, no-one seemed certain of the exact location of New Edinburgh or Fort St Andrew in Caledonia Bay. Then, in December 1978, she read in the newspaper that the two locations had been unearthed by archaeologists and Young Explorers on Phase 1 of Operation Drake.

By then Cathy had heard that she and six other Scots had been selected for Phase 2. She was being sponsored by the patron of Operation Drake himself, HRH The Prince of Wales. She was to spend three months on the expedition which would include, amongst many other projects, a complete excavation of the old site of Caledonia which had been left undisturbed for 280 years. No wonder she couldn't wait to be flown out to Central America to join the expedition.

By the time I arrived in Panama it was mid-January. I had flown from the grey skies and drizzle of Edinburgh into the brilliant sunshine and blue skies of New Edinburgh on the Panamanian coast. I left behind all my winter woollies to face sweltering heat, sandflies and mosquitoes. We strolled among the palm trees in T-shirts and shorts. It all seemed like a strange dream.

Mark Horton, the archaeologist in charge of the excavation, gave us a tour around the site and pointed out some rocks sticking out of the topsoil which he thought were the ramparts of Fort St Andrew. Later he showed us some musket balls, pottery, clay pipes and brandy bottles which had already been unearthed. These made quite an impression on us Scots. It was hard to imagine that they had been used by our countrymen over 200 years ago.

The work started with us trying to clear the remainder of the site so that the archaeologists could sift the earth. We bashed away with our machetes – it was very strenuous in

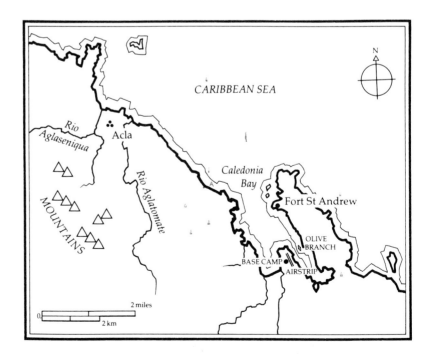

that heat, especially when cutting down big trees – then slashed away at the foliage.

It was hard work, but good fun all the same. Sifting the earth looking for artefacts was even harder: it demanded such patience. It was dangerous too. Great coconuts kept dropping from the palm trees above. In the end, we decided to wear helmets to protect ourselves.

I was at the site when several interesting things were discovered. Firstly, we found what looked like a flint from an old musket. It must have been imported from Scotland because there was no rock like that anywhere on the coast. Then there was the coin. It was a wee coin not much larger than a finger nail. All the experts excitedly clamoured around, then turned it over slowly. It had some markings on it. They all looked very puzzled. 'Let's have a look,' I said. They handed it over for my inspection. 'Aach, that's the badge of the City of Edinburgh. Look, that wee castle in the middle of the coin, that's Edinburgh Castle.' They were all very surprised.

I was also in camp the day a couple of the diving team came ashore and said they thought they'd found the sunken Scots galleon, the *Olive Branch*. The *Olive Branch* was destroyed by fire in 1699 when one of the crew, a cooper,

Above Diane Newton (New Zealand), Nicholas Hopkins (England) and Ricardo Pasco (Panama) excavate the ramparts of Fort St Andrew in Caledonia Bay, Panama.

Below A 17th-century coin decorated with the coat of arms of the city of Edinburgh. It was left behind by Scottish settlers who deserted the site of Fort St Andrew in 1700.

went in search of brandy. He was carrying a candle which somehow set the ship alight. It sank without trace. The divers had had quite a tough time. They had had to dive into murky waters where the current and underwater swell pushed them against the sharp coral. The diving platform was a very large inflatable boat which surged and heaved on the choppy waves. It must have been very unpleasant.

They brought with them a heavily-encrusted lump from the bowels of the ship. When it was broken apart it revealed a collection of clay pipes with a sort of hallmark on the bowls. The pipes were identical to those which had been found on the site of Fort St Andrew. Other items from the ship proved that the wreck was that of the *Maid of Perth* which was renamed the *Olive Branch* when it sailed from Scotland for Central America in 1698.

The 25th January is 'Burns Night' and as we had a piper from the Scots Guards and a lot of Scots in camp, we decided to celebrate. Scots all over the world meet on this date to read the poetry of their greatest poet, Robbie Burns. A few of us climbed onto the bluff 30 metres above the camp, carrying a flag pole and the old flag of Scotland – the red lion of Scotland on a yellow background. When we looked down we could see expedition members and guests from Panama City, who had arrived for the celebrations, scurrying around like ants. Then we raised the flag over the old Scottish settlement, the first time for 280 years. At that moment came the skirl of the bagpipes. We could see our piper, Robbie Little, 150 metres below us. Dressed in full ceremonial costume, with kilt and sporran, he marched along the sand beneath the palm trees to a small jetty which stretched out into Caledonia Bay. There he played a sad lament. I almost wept.

That night we had a great feast. Haggis, a traditional Scots dish of sheep's lights minced with oatmeal, had been flown in from Scotland. We toasted Robbie Burns in whisky and then toasted each guest. More toasts followed. Later we went out on to the beach and performed some Scottish country dances. It was a marvellous evening.

Nevertheless the most memorable experience of those re-markable three months was the Balboa Patrol. We planned to walk from the Atlantic Ocean to the Pacific across the Darien Isthmus following the supposed route of Balboa.

In August 1513, Vasco Nunez de Balboa set out to cross the Isthmus of Panama with 190 heavily-armed Spaniards and a large number of Indians. Four months later he returned a hero, laden with treasure. He was named as the discoverer

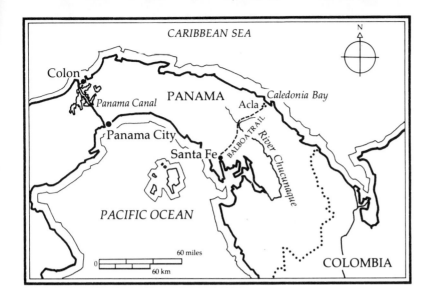

of the Pacific Ocean. On his return, he founded the town of Acla which was thought to be a few kilometres north of the base camp at Caledonia Bay. But his success was short-lived as he and five of his lieutenants were executed by a jealous governor. Gradually Acla disappeared until all trace of it had gone – then it was discovered by archaeologists with Operation Drake.

George Thurstan, an ex Marine-Commando, had picked the team very carefully. We all had to go through a strict medical test, and several volunteers were turned down because they were not as fit as he wanted. On 25 February we set off from Acla on the Atlantic coast. There were twenty-four in the party, twelve of us YE's. Three YE's were girls. We expected and received no favouritism. There were also five members of the *Guardia Nationale* from Panama City and a Choco Indian guide with the delightful name of Jesus Zuleta.

We had the minimum of equipment and food because we had over 180 kilometres of very tough country to cross: thick jungle, a mountain range, rivers and a rugged dry area which had scarcely ever been crossed before. The jungle was very dense. It wasn't easy to map read and arrange for fresh provisions of food, yet Jesus kept us supplied with fresh turkey, wild pig and, on one occasion, monkey and snake. We had the usual problems of foot-rot, ticks and the occasional attacks of diarrhoea but, in the circumstances, things were going quite well.

But, as Robbie Burns once said 'the best laid schemes of mice and men, gang oft a gley'. Things started to go wrong

Far from any river, the patrol had to ration water strictly. Here Cathy Davies pours precious water into Denise Wilson's (England) water bottle.

on the eleventh day after we crossed the Chucanaque River, the last main river before the dry zone. We all had two full water bottles, but we drank as little as possible. That night we found no water. Most people had only one full bottle left, and some of us shared out our water ration with those who had less self-control. It was hard that night.

I can remember lying in my hammock after a very small evening meal. Everyone had gone to bed early. I looked up at the moon and thought, 'Will I be able to get up in the morning, put on a rucksack and face the heat of the day with only one bottle of water?' It was a troubled night. I wondered how I would react.

Next morning we started at dawn. I hadn't touched a drop of water in the night, but I knew some had drunk a fair bit.

At midday, we found a small pool. Carefully we filtered the filthy water, boiled it for a few minutes, then popped in a couple of sterilizing tablets. Each person filled two bottles. On we went. Again no water that night.

The next day was terrible. We had to cut our way through thick undergrowth which crossed the track. We were sweating like pigs and dying for a taste of cold clear water. Just before midday Rick Gustavsson, the Canadian film-man, began to stagger. We shared out his kit between us but soon he wasn't even able to walk straight. Then we had to half carry him. He was obviously very ill. A little later, we stopped for half a cup of tea and a nibble of a biscuit. Rick couldn't keep anything down and was violently sick. We all leaned against our rucksacks absolutely knackered. There wasn't a smile in sight.

Then one of the *Guardia* suddenly keeled over and began to vomit. George Thurstan must have realised it was no good trying to continue. Both sick men had very high temperatures and their hearts were beating like crazy. George got onto the radio and asked for a helicopter to come and get the sick men out. He also asked for water to be dropped to the patrol.

One problem remained: how to clear an area large enough for a helicopter landing pad. I can still remember that terrible feeling of apathy – everyone was so tired. Then George said, 'Right, we've got to clear a landing site. Everyone up.' Amazingly, everyone did, and we began to feel more cheerful as we got on with the job. Some of the trees had trunks 2 metres thick and were 30 or 40 metres tall. Cutting the clearing with only machetes was very hard. Our hands were so soft. Everyone got blisters. Worst of all, we sweated heavily and so lost a lot of water from our bodies. Trees were falling in all directions and I was nearly hit by an enormous trunk. Suddenly two YE's keeled over, they just seemed to give up and collapse.

By now, George had sent out an SOS on the radio to the main headquarters in Panama City. He had been told that the helicopter should reach us in a couple of hours. He had been asked to put out smoke signals so that the pilots could find us. It was a terrible effort just to build those fires. At 4.45 p.m., the time at which the helicopters were expected, we lit the fires, but they were too small to be seen. One of the *Guardia* then shinned up one of the tallest trees with a couple of red smoke flares. The rest of us listened for the sound of whirling propellers. But there was nothing. Hours passed.

Cathy Davies helps to clear a landing zone for the helicopter which had been called to airlift out three sick members of the Balboa patrol. The patrol was following Balboa's route across the Darien Isthmus from the Atlantic to the Pacific Ocean.

With only centimetres to spare on either side of the rotor blades, the helicopter prepares to lift out the sick members of the Balboa patrol.

Nothing. By this time the fires were almost out, with only a small spiral of smoke rising up to the level of the canopy. We tried to put up an orange marker balloon, but we didn't have enough water to pour onto the chemicals to make the gas to fill it. Urine didn't work either.

It was getting dark so we decided to put up our hammocks. Suddenly there was a whoop from Luis Murillo up the tree. He let off one of the grenades. Everyone stopped what they were doing and looked up at the great plume of red smoke rising in the darkening sky. Soon a large American army helicopter was hovering above the clearing at canopy level. The pilot was obviously trying to decide whether it was safe to land amongst the tree stumps. By now, we were leaping up and down, waving like crazy. Then all of a sudden the helicopter disappeared. It had moved off to get a magnetic fix on the patrol's location.

But it didn't return. Later we found out that in the gathering gloom it had lost sight of us completely. For ten long minutes we were out of contact, and out of sight. Our spirits sagged. Eventually, however, the helicopter was contacted on the radio and guided in our direction.

To our intense relief the helicopter appeared above us once again. A winch was lowered and Rick was slowly lifted into the helicopter. It hovered a moment as the pilot sent a message over the radio to tell us that another helicopter would come out early next morning to collect the rest of the sick and to drop in water. It was a long, dry night.

Next morning, a helicopter flew out from Panama, but it couldn't find us, although we continually sent spirals of smoke above the canopy by placing wet leaves on fires. We were soon exhausted again. Then another of the *Guardia* fell sick and joined the other two who by now were looking very ill indeed. It took four hours before the helicopter arrived to fly them to Gorgas Hospital in Panama City.

Just before the helicopter left, the crew dropped six jerry cans of precious water. It was the best drink I've ever had in my life. We were able to drink as much as we could swallow. It was delicious. I drank an army mugful in one go.

That night, the eighteenth of the patrol, we all felt stronger. The crisis was over. The next morning, with two cutters up front, we carried on. Eventually we came to a dried-up river bed and followed it to the main river. Here we found damp water patches and, lower down, some wee muddy puddles. One pool had a fish, floating belly upwards. Carefully we filtered the water through a handkerchief into our bottles and added the sterilising tablets.

We walked steadily, hoping to reach the main Pan-American highway, but after twelve hours' continuous marching we still hadn't got there. Even so, we all felt quite festive that evening. We knew that sometime tomorrow we would hit the main highway and then walk down to Santa Fé. We had a great meal of turkey and rice before turning into our hammocks. All our energy seemed to have returned.

Next day – the twentieth of the patrol – we reached the highway and completed the last 10 kilometres of our patrol. After three weeks in the gloom of the jungle, during which we had covered a distance of 180 kilometres, the glare of the sun was blinding. It was an extraordinary feeling to think we were on our way to Santa Fé, to civilisation, human beings, houses, trucks, and cold clear water. Everyone felt a real sense of achievement. We'd been through it, but we'd kept going and taken it all in our stride. We'd found the strength to keep going. It was fantastic; we felt great.

How Balboa and his men did it in 1513, I'll never know. They wore armour and actually took a boat with them to reassemble on the other side! They had no mosquito nets, malaprim tablets for malaria, jungle boots, hammocks or lightweight rations – they must have had a hell of a time.

When we eventually got back to the Base Camp at

David French (England) is helped across the clearing in the jungle by Chye Ong (Malaysia) and Irving Bennett (Panama) to the waiting helicopter.

Caledonia Bay, I was handed a letter from my sponsor, Prince Charles. It was written in his own hand on Windsor Castle paper and signed *Yours, Charles*. Except for getting across the Isthmus, this was the most thrilling thing that had ever happened to me. It showed that Prince Charles was taking a personal interest in the whole project, and particularly in Darien. At one point in the letter he said, 'Hope you have not suffered any irreparable damage as a result of your exposure to all those infernal creeping creatures'. I thought of the horrible ticks and black river flies we had suffered on the Chucanaque River. My face was covered in bites. He finished his letter 'Your sponsor could not be more pleased that you have found it a valuable exerience.' I most certainly had, and it was all thanks to him.

Although it had been tough, I was pleased I'd been able to do it. It changed my whole attitude to so many things. I got back to my camp bed after sleeping in a hammock for a month. There alongside it was my large kitbag, yet I had survived quite happily living out of one wee rucksack. I thought to myself, 'What do I need all that stuff for?' I really did. It suddenly brought back to me what was really essential in life. For us on that trip, it was water. It didn't matter if our clothes didn't fit, if we ran short of food. All that mattered was water.

Now I've returned to Britain, I see people getting all worked up about unimportant things. To me the most important things are my friends. My experiences on Operation Drake have made me rethink such a lot of things. For a start I know just how lucky I am – especially to have marched across the Darien Isthmus to the Pacific Ocean in the steps of Balboa.

On her return to Scotland, Cathy Davies went to university to study Spanish, French and German. She was accepted as a member of staff on Phase 5 of Operation Drake, and since 1981 has helped organise adventure training courses for young people during her vacations.

PHASE 3   April 1979 – July 1979

Across the Broad Pacific

Gavin Whitelaw *South Africa*

I don't remember much about the first few days. But I do remember being woken up one night at midnight. Feeling desperately ill, I staggered onto the deck for my first stint of watch duty. The swell had got stronger and the diesel fumes from the engine exhaust smelt terrible. All those stories about sea sickness were true. I felt like curling up in a corner and dying.

Gavin Whitelaw, an eighteen-year-old South African, was working as a bank clerk in Johannesburg when he was selected to join Operation Drake. Although he had been around Africa and even gone on an expedition to Iceland, he had never been on a large sailing ship before. He volunteered for Phase 3 because he thought it would be marvellous to sail across the Pacific from Panama to Fiji. He would also get a chance to visit the Charles Darwin Research Station on the Galapagos Islands. He had wanted to visit the Station for a long time. He hoped to study zoology and geography at university when he returned to South Africa.

I had no idea the Pacific would be like this. I had always imagined it to be smooth and placid like the Panama Canal, which we had sailed through the day before.

The Panama Canal was completed in 1914, some fifteen years after the Suez Canal. Before it was built, men like Francis Drake had to sail an extra 4,000 kilometres around the southern tip of South America to reach the Pacific Ocean. The 64-kilometre long Panama Canal took ten years to build at the cost of many lives. Today, about 1,500 ships enter the Canal every year, each of which has to take a pilot aboard to help negotiate the series of locks across the Canal.

The Canal pilot had come aboard at Colon. A series of three locks took us about 20 metres above sea level to Gatun Lake – the longest part of the Canal. The locks were lined with concrete and had huge steel doors. Along the top of the lock sides, small engines ran on rails. These 'donkeys', as they were called, were used to pull larger ships through the locks.

On Gatun Lake there was little wind and the water seemed to move sluggishly. The bush-covered shores shimmered in the intense heat. It was easy to see why thousands of men had died building the Canal. On the western side of the Panamanian Isthmus, another three locks took us down to sea level, where we drew alongside the wharf in the Port of Balboa.

After we had taken on more supplies of food and water, we sailed a further 500 kilometres to San Pedro in Costa Rica. I disembarked with half of the twenty-four YE's. The remainder of the crew sailed 15 kilometres north to Drake's Bay, where we planned to rendezvous with them on foot the next day. Guided by four Costa Ricans, we walked north along the coastline. We passed through cool, dark forests where monkeys chattered and shrieked, and through overgrown plantations where we picked and ate bananas and mangoes. We swam in cold rivers. It was idyllic. We reached Drake's Bay after nightfall and saw the *Eye of the Wind* lying offshore. She was a beautiful sight.

Our first project was to do a biological survey of the shore of Drake's Bay. Small sections of the beach were marked out in squares and the animal and plant life in each section examined and noted. We found some extraordinary and often very amusing creatures. The rock pools and river mouth in particular revealed a variety of colourful animals. Trish Holdway recorded the results of the extensive survey for a report to be given to the Costa Rican authorities.

Dr Trish Holdway, the ship's marine biologist, examines plankton samples in the laboratory on the Eye of the Wind. *This laboratory was specially constructed for Operation Drake.*

We then weighed anchor* and set off westwards for Cocos Island. There was a fairly good following wind when we left, so for two days we really sailed. Our clumsy attempts at handling the sails became more practised and our self-confidence grew. Then the wind changed and we had to use the engine. Soon Cocos Island rose above the horizon, a rugged green mountain surrounded by azure blue shallows. We anchored at Chatham Bay in water so clear, that we could see the sharks and fish darting about below us.

Cocos is a lonely palm-fringed island 600 kilometres off the coast of Panama. Two hundred years ago, a schooner called the Mary Dyer *was wrecked on its shores. It was filled with treasure and, for a long time, people believed that it may have been hidden on the island. Pirates such as Bonito, Thomson and Henry Morgan also used to rest up and collect water there. It has long been rumoured that Morgan buried fabulous treasures on the island and, in 1888, a man named Gissler was sent from Costa Rica to look for the treasure. He searched for eighteen years but never found it.*

Soon after we had dropped anchor in Chatham Bay, Frank Esson, a watch leader, led a band of YE's in search of an Allied aircraft that had crashed on the island in 1942. I followed soon afterwards in a second group led by another watch leader, Robert Clinton. We were to explore the island.

Chatham Bay beach consists of stones, pebbles and large rocks. There are carvings on the rocks which are 300 years old. From the beach, the island rises almost vertically out of the sea before it flattens out at the top. We climbed through cool forests until, slipping and sliding down a thick red mud slope, we arrived at Wafer Bay.

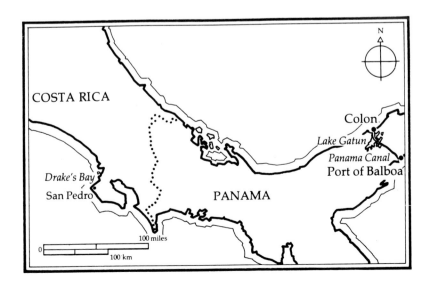

Julie Barlow (Australia), Bill Hargroves (USA), Cathy Lawrence (Canada), Diane Patterson (NZ) and Miranda Kichenside (England) take a last fresh-water shower on Cocos Island before crossing the Pacific Ocean.

A group of Costa Rican *Guardia* lived in two huts near Wafer Bay beach. Close to the huts were the remnants of the once enormous coconut palm groves after which the island was named. The *Guardia* generously took us in, gave us a bed each and some of their excellent food. Next day, one of them helped us explore Wafer Bay. We climbed waterfalls and crawled through underground tunnels. I'm sure many of us were thinking about that missing pirate treasure.

In the early afternoon, we returned to the huts where we met Frank's exhausted 'swamp rats'. They'd had a hard slog in appalling weather. They'd even spent a freezing night huddled together for warmth on a mountainside. But they'd found the missing areoplane.

The *Eye of the Wind* sailed for the Galapagos Islands that evening. On 21 May we crossed the Equator and hove-to* for the traditional 'crossing the line' ceremony. The weather was perfect. 'King Neptune', and his 'Queen' and a 'Fish' attendant appeared over the bow. King Neptune's hench-men smeared us with a kind of foul-smelling paste and Robert Clinton – the 'Lawyer' – read out all the faults and mistakes we had committed on board the *Eye of the Wind*. One by one we were dunked in a makeshift pool by the 'Fish', alias Tiger Timbs the Mate. In the end, everyone was

When the Eye of the Wind *crossed the Equator, Dianne Patterson (NZ) was initiated into the 'Most Noble Order of the Deep' by King Neptune and Davey Jones. This ancient 'crossing the line' ceremony goes back to early seafaring days.*

hurled into the ducking pool – including Captain Mike Kichenside, our skipper. It was great fun.

The Galapagos Islands are unique. Their terrain is harsh and forbidding, yet they provide a home for an incredible variety of weird and wonderful creatures that are found nowhere else in the world. One of these is a huge tortoise ('galapagos' means 'tortoise' in Spanish). Separate subspecies have even developed on separate islands. It was on these islands that Charles Darwin began to formulate his theory of evolution.

But when trading ships started to visit the Galapagos, they brought with them rats and dogs, which harmed the islands' animal and bird life. Many are now threatened with extinction. At the Charles Darwin Research Station, on the island of Santa Cruz, scientists from all over the world gather to try

A display of aggression by two giant tortoises on Santa Cruz, one of the Galapagos Islands. These animals could be over 100 years old.

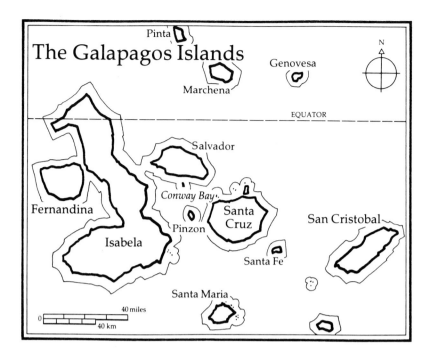

and save them. We were asked to help with two projects: to find wild goats on Marchena and San Salvador Islands and to try and capture land iguanas in Conway Bay on the western side of Santa Cruz.

The first taste we had of the real Galapagos was on a small island off Santa Cruz. For many of us, this island proved to be the highlight of our Galapagos visit. The tameness of the animals and birds ashore was quite extraordinary. We were able to get extremely close to animals that previously we'd only seen in wildlife books.

In the afternoon, we saw a group of sea-lions swimming offshore and decided to join them. They swam with incredible grace and speed; some came up to us and put their noses against the glass of our goggles. They were so appealing that soon almost all the crew were swimming amongst them. But after a while a bull sea-lion became rather aggressive towards us and we decided to leave them in peace.

Marchena was different. The island rose up from coal black beaches to the crater of a volcano. The slopes of the mountain were covered with silvery-white grass and palo-santo trees, trees which are covered with a lace-like moss. From the lip of the volcano, the crater floor looked forbidding. It was a flat stretch of black lava, broken only by hillocks. There was a 'burnt toast' atmosphere about the place.

We split into three groups and set off in different directions to try and find some goats to count. My group

Left *Twenty metres above a rolling deck, two young explorers carefully make their way along the yard to release the lower topsail during the Pacific Ocean crossing.*

Below *In gale-force winds, young explorers receive instruction on how to handle the sails of the* Eye of the Wind *during the crossing of the Atlantic Ocean.*

Dr Trish Holdway, marine biologist, conducts a survey
of the plants and coral on Vesuvius Reef in Indonesian
waters. The Eye of the Wind is anchored alongside.

Above Collecting leaf
samples from the aerial
walkway in the canopy of
the Panamanian rain
forest. The walkway was
suspended 35 metres above
the ground.

Left *During their survey of the proposed Morowali Nature Reserve in Sulawesi, young explorers fill their water bottles with water squeezed from lichen moss in the Tambusisi moss forest.*

Rendille tribesmen load the pack camels early in the morning in preparation for another day's trek across the Koroli Desert in northern Kenya.

went down into the crater where it was very hot, even though it was still early. The rocks underfoot were sharp and rough and cracked continually, making a curious glass-like crunch. All day we plodded across the crater but found no goats and little sign of any other life. It was a great relief to get back to the shore. Sailors must have had Marchena in mind when they described the Galapagos archipelago as 'godforsaken'.

Four days after leaving the Galapagos we picked up the trade winds again. The wind was on our beam* and our daily distances increased dramatically as we got further into the trade wind belt. We hoped that we would beat the 323 kilometres sailing record. At night, the sea was particularly impressive as the bow* waves roared beneath us and the masts towered above. When we ran into minor squalls, the wet canvas glistened in the starlight above us.

During the day we worked hard at chipping, sanding and varnishing. The deck houses* were sanded down and re-varnished; metal fittings were chipped free of rust and then painted. Soon the *Eye of the Wind* began to shine in the sun as rust and discoloured wood disappeared. We were running before the wind now, often rolling hopelessly in the swell. Several times plates and pots crashed down from their fastenings in the galley. The deck was continually awash with water, making it impossible to paint. Huge patches of paint flaked off and exposed the bare metal beneath.

But not every day was like this. Many were hot and sunny and we cooled ourselves with seawater collected in buckets overboard. Then we did little work and just talked quietly amongst ourselves. There was hardly any noise except for the occasional crack of the sails. Further for'ard* there would be the odd splash as one of the 'galley slaves' threw dirty dishwater overboard.

Once a week in the evening, we all gathered on the poop deck* to swop jokes and stories. We felt really close to one another. After fifty-seven days out of sight of land, we had become one big family. Each of us was made to feel essential to the ship's company. It was a marvellous feeling.

Suddenly, we saw Tahiti, lying like a huge emerald in the deep blue ocean. As we got closer we revelled in the lush-ness of the greens, reds and yellows. The smell of wet earth, of the bush, of human habitation was a sensation which had almost been forgotten during the past three weeks.

Several of us hired a jeep and drove around the island enjoying the sights and sounds of land. We bought long

French loaves, fresh cream and cheese which were non-existent on board. It was marvellous to take long walks on solid ground again.

Once we left Tahiti the weather changed. It became unpredictable and we had to work the sails nearly all the time. The squalls were violent. One was so bad that we only set two sails and doubled the watch. At other times, the sea was a flat calm and we were able to hove-to and swim.

There were lots of parties, both spontaneous and planned. We all dressed in outrageous clothes for a John Travolta 50's Night, and had to keep absolute silence during a Trappist Monks' Night. Then there was a fo'csle* party when we crammed the entire ship's company into the tiny fo'csle, and Trish Holdway made a cake in the shape of the *Eye of the Wind*. We even celebrated American Independence Day with pancakes and syrup for breakfast.

This was the last leg of our trip; the atmosphere was tinged with sadness as we neared Fiji and realised that we would soon be parted. On 18 July we approached Suva, the capital of Fiji. Our entrance to Suva harbour at the end of our three-month phase was one of the golden moments of the voyage. After a ferocious squall the night before, we were buoyed up with tension, lack of sleep and pure excitement.

The wind was still strong so we shot through the passage in the reef at the entrance of the harbour, and then furled sail as we glided closer to the wharf. At last, we drew gently alongside. For us the voyage was over.

At times Operation Drake pushed me to my physical and mental limits. I won't forget the times I climbed 30 metres from the deck to the top of the main mast in a storm to unfurl the Operation Drake flag, which had got caught up. Once I had just got down to the deck, and looked up to see the flag all wrapped up again . . . so back I had to climb. Nor will I forget the excitement of edging the beautiful square-rigged ship between perilous reefs of coral. Oh, there were a million and one highlights, which I will always cherish. But above all, I will never forget the friends I made, friends from all over the world who sailed with me amongst those fantastic Pacific islands.

Gavin Whitelaw returned to South Africa to take a BSc in zoology and geography at the University of Witwatersrand. In the winter of 1980, he went to England to see the arrival of the Eye of the Wind *in London and to meet many of the friends he had made on Operation Drake.*

The hold of the Eye of the Wind *was converted into a saloon for Young Explorers to relax in when they were off watch. Here Cathy Lawrence (Canada), Linda Batt-Rawden (England) and Scott Brown (USA) listen to Guy Clarkson (Canada) and Jamie Howard (USA) on the guitar.*

Hurricane Relief and River-Running

Nyoli Waghorn *New Zealand*

trees had all lost their leaves and those still upright were bent at a crazy angle. I could see where the wind had swept uphill and flattened everything. The seashore was lined with debris: seaweed, driftwood, shells and coconuts. It was a mess. I couldn't see any buildings on the islands, yet I could see smoke rising above the vegetation. Obviously the villagers were still living there, hidden from sight.

I hadn't seen the effects of a hurricane before. Four months ago, the island of Moala had been laid bare;

Twenty-two year old Nyoli was living in a small hut on the west coast of the southern island of New Zealand when she heard about Operation Drake. She was working part-time as a supply nurse at the local hospital. In her spare time, she 'pottered about' the mountains and caves, went fishing and looked after her small garden. As soon as she heard she had been selected for the expedition, however, she realised that somehow she would have to earn some extra money. So she moved to Christchurch and began work in the airforce base hospital at Wigram. It was the staff there who organised several raffles which brought in enough cash to allow her to go.

As our landing craft approached the shores of Moala, in Fiji, we could see groups of people on the beach pushing out small wooden punts and one larger dugout-canoe powered by an outboard engine. They tethered the punts behind the canoe and set out towards us. As they approached we could hear laughing and singing – everyone seemed so excited. When the craft eventually came alongside, we lowered our gear into the canoe and dropped over the side into the waiting punts.

This caused quite a sensation. There were five girls in our group, and we were all wearing shorts. Later, we found out that women in Fiji don't wear shorts; they have to keep their legs covered from waist to ankles with a brightly-coloured garment called a *sulu*. What's more, our legs were still very white as we hadn't seen much sun yet. So when the islanders saw white women climbing out of the punts, carrying large packs and wearing shorts, they could hardly believe it. They pointed at us and laughed and laughed.

Everybody was very friendly. We were met by the chief and elders of the village, then taken to one of their huts. They had kindly organised a special *sevu sevu* ceremony for us. This is only laid on for a very important occasion. The ceremony begins with everyone sitting cross-legged in a large circle. Places in this circle are allocated by the chief of the village, and the closer to him you sit, the greater the honour. In the centre stands a large bowl containing *kava*, a ceremonial drink made from the pounded roots of a young yaqona tree mixed with water. The village chief instructs one of his men to serve his guests with a *bilo* of *kava*. (A *bilo* is a drinking cup made from half of a highly polished coconut.) The chief points to guests in turn who are then offered the *kava*. Once a guest has taken the *bilo* the server has to clap his hands once. The guest then drinks the liquid – you are not supposed to sip it but drink it straight down in one long gulp. When the bowl is empty and before it is handed back, the server says *maca* (pronounced 'matha') and claps three times.

At first, *kava* tastes rather brackish – it even looks like muddy water. But by the time your turn comes round again, you're keen to take another drink. *Kava* makes your mouth slightly numb and makes you feel a little light-headed. After a while you really begin to get a taste for it. I took some powdered *kava* home with me to New Zealand to try it out on my friends. But I'm not sure they liked it quite as much as I did.

The young people of Moala Island, Fiji, help the Young Explorers lay the foundations for a new school. The old one was destroyed by Hurricane Meli. Many of the palm trees were bent sideways by the force of the wind.

Opposite After work, the Young Explorers were given a traditional meal of rice, fish, root vegetables and fruit by Moala Islanders.

Once the *sevu sevu* ceremony was over, we were directed to the houses where we were to stay overnight. In the centre of the village, the women had prepared a great feast for us. A brightly-coloured cloth had been laid on the ground, and on this was a selection of steaming bowls of food – shellfish, vegetables, fish in sauce, pork, chicken and many other delicacies. We couldn't wait to tuck in. It was so good we thought it was a special feast to celebrate our arrival, but later we discovered that there was a meal like this every day. Marvellous!

In the afternoon, we made a start on one of our jobs – rebuilding the school which had been flattened by the hurricane. The building materials were lying on the beach, so we spent the rest of the day lugging them up to the field. Fortunately, the children had been given a day off school to help.

We had three buildings to put up, one on the hill and two on the field. Unfortunately, the field was very uneven and stony and we only had four spades and shovels plus a couple of wheelbarrows to do the job. To make it more difficult, there were some enormous boulders, three or four of which must have weighed several tonnes. We had to prise each one out with a crowbar, then lift it with ropes onto a sort of wooden sledge. We then dragged the sledge – some pushing,

others pulling – across the playing field and beach and into the sea. Boy, did we get hot!

I am a nurse and as a result got to know the islanders in a slightly different way from the other YE's. Because I visited each household and offered medical help, and also tried to learn Fijian, I was accepted into every family. One of the most important men in the village even asked me if he could become my Fijian father. When I accepted, he gave me a piece of carved cross, which had been in his family for many generations. I felt very honoured.

The villagers had been so kind and welcoming that when the time came to leave, we were all very sorry to go. On the evening before our departure, the women dressed in their multi-coloured garments, put on their necklaces of shells and flowers and serenaded us. They even sprinkled talcum powder in our hair, which apparently is another great privilege and honour. We danced and sang well into the night. I only wished that the night could have gone on for ever.

Next morning, we were all very sad. At 10 a.m. the masts of the Prime Minister's yacht appeared on the horizon. It had come to collect us and return us to Suva, the capital of Fiji. After last-minute hugs and lots of tears, we were given gifts of shells, mats, fans and carvings, before we were led through the surf into the punts. The rest of the village stood at the water's edge, waving and singing a song of farewell. Slowly we were paddled out to the waiting ship with the music of the guitar and singing voices echoing in our ears. I

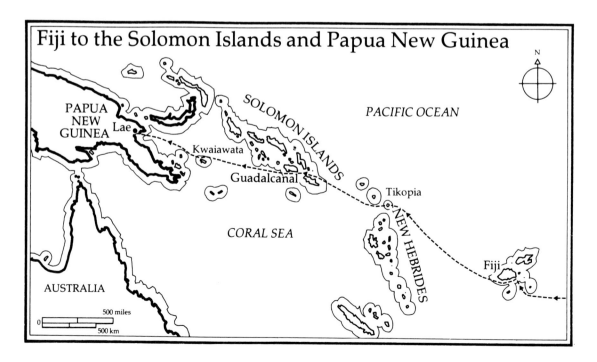

Fiji to the Solomon Islands and Papua New Guinea

Wizz Gambier (England)
dances with villagers of
Kwaiwata in the
Marshall Bennett
Islands.

doubt if there was a dry eye amongst us as we gave our last waves to the little knot of people standing on the shore.

From Suva, we went to Papua New Guinea, where a completely different experience was awaiting us. On the way, we island-hopped through the Solomon Islands, visited war memorials in Guadalcanal and even worked as extras in the film 'The Blue Lagoon'. Columbia Films hired the *Eye of the Wind*, renamed her the *Northumberland* and used her for the opening shots. We were filmed clambering up and down the rigging – and were paid for doing it!

On 5 September, we sighted the east coast of Papua New Guinea – or PNG as it is called locally. With all fifteen sails set, we made an impressive sight on our arrival in Lae harbour. On the quay a *sing sing* had been organised for us, and a large crowd was waiting for us to land. But our mail had also arrived and it was difficult to concentrate on the dancing when we had precious letters to read.

After an official welcome at the quay, we were loaded into yellow pick-ups and driven to Lae Lodge, the HQ of Operation Drake PNG. Outside a couple of bungalows on stilts, which were festooned with aerials and notices , we were given a complete briefing and told exactly what we were to do during our remaining month with Operation Drake. There were ten projects to choose from. Before anything else, we were to all take part in a seven-day jungle acquaintance course.

Our course began with an introduction to poisonous plants, animals, centipedes, snakes, leeches, ants – and a hundred and one other nasty creatures found in the jungle. For a simple New Zealander, who had never experienced any danger in the bush, this was rather a frightening experience. Of course, it poured with rain when we wanted to cook our evening meal, and to our horror we discovered that the plastic fly sheets which we slung on a rope over our hammocks were not really long enough to keep out the rain. Perhaps we were doing it all wrong; in any case, the rain poured in.

The next day we used machetes to cut our way through the jungle on several compass-bearing exercises. The person who set the course must have had a weird sense of humour because we were often up to our waists in swampy marsh. When we returned to the campsite, Sergeant Major Tiki of the PNG Defence Force showed us how to cook a pig in a *mumu*. He dug a deep hole in the earth and put into it a selection of large red-hot stones which had been taken from a nearby fire. He covered the hot stones with banana leaves, placed the meat on top, covered it with more leaves and then put several more hot stones on top. The whole *mumu* was then covered with earth to make a complete oven. We allowed it to cook for three to four hours before the stones were rolled back to reveal tender cooked pork. It was delicious.

By the time we had completed our week in the jungle we felt much more confident and self-reliant. We were not frightened by the sounds of the jungle – the rustlings, cheepings, croakings, and chirrupings as the night animals and insects went on their way. We felt much happier carrying large packs in the bush, navigating, erecting a camp site and even operating the radio. In fact, we felt we could tackle anything.

But I didn't expect river-running to be quite so varied and difficult. I was one of five YE's to navigate the Watut River in two rubber inflatable boats. The party was led by Jim Masters, an experienced explorer, who had navigated both the Blue Nile and Zaire Rivers. As well as Jim, we were lucky to have Yogi Thami, a Nepalese professional river-runner, to teach us the skills of the helmsman. He sat on an aluminium frame in the centre of the raft, and used oars to turn the bows of the raft past obstacles. We took it in turns to learn how to do this.

At first the river was deceptively smooth and fast-running, flowing through a series of shallows past several villages. At the water's edge, we could see men panning for gold. On each side of the river was dense jungle and spreading branches from which hanging vines trailed into the water. There were several logs jammed into the banks. It was only when we ran into one of these that we appreciated the full force of the water. But after a short time, we managed to control the craft by deft strokes of the oars and furious paddling.

Village children run the rapids on gummis *(large inflated lorry inner tubes).*

Usually, we drifted past the villages unobserved, but sometimes the local children ran excitedly to the water's edge, waved and shouted, then ran off to collect their *gummis* (inflated inner-tubes of tractor wheels or lorry wheels). The youngsters threw them in the water, sat in the centre, and used a banana frond as a paddle. As they bounced ahead of us into the rapids, shouting with glee, we felt a little embarrassed by all our fancy gear.

We were usually on the river by 7 a.m. As we travelled further, the river got deeper and faster. We had to negotiate more and more rocks in the centre of the river as the sides of the Watut became steeper and steeper.

You can hear the roar of a rapid well before you see it. Then you see the tell-tale haze of spray rising like smoke above the lip of the rapid. (The lip is the small waterfall which marks the start of the rapids.) If possible, you pull into the side so that the helmsman can get a better look at the obstacles ahead. When he returns, you receive your instructions and push off into the fast-flowing river. As you approach the lip, the raft gathers speed and the people in the bows get their paddles ready. Your heart beats fast in excitement. The helmsman pulls frantically at the oars to ensure that the bows approach the drop ahead at a right angle and dead in the centre. He continually shouts commands above the roar of the water – 'Paddle left . . . Back paddle right . . . Steady . . . Here we go . . .'

By now all fear has gone as you sweep over the lip and

down the V formation of water ahead. Everything happens so quickly. Rocks flash by on both sides. Then the raft slams into the large wave at the tip of the V. Bows lurch crazily upwards. You are covered in spray as the bows crash down onto the next wave, then up you go again, crash, crash, crash. Sometimes you duck as a great curve of green water pours over the bows. You grab hold of the safety line before you are sucked over the side of the raft into the churning water. Suddenly, you are through it. There are whoops of excitement and everyone laughs or grins with relief and exhilaration. Incredible.

By the end of the second day we were really working as a team and enjoying every minute of it. But on the third we had a nasty shock. As we came over the lip of a rapid we saw a large black shiny rock jutting up just ahead of us. We had a choice of two routes, both very narrow. The helmsman had to make a split-second decision. First he told us to paddle to the left, then he changed his mind and directed us through the right-hand channel. It was too late. The rock came up at us with alarming speed. We dug into the water with our paddles, but the right tube of our raft hit the rock broadside with a loud 'thwack'. Slowly it began to rise up. The noise of the water was deafening. Our helmsman shouted to us to leap onto the right-hand tube to force it down with our weight. Water was now pouring into the craft over the submerged tube. We were too slow. Our raft was firmly pancaked around the boulder. I just managed to hold onto the safety line, as the water tried to drag me from the raft. Slowly I inched up the side and onto the rock.

We must have spent a quarter of an hour trying to push and pull the raft free – two of the crew on the rock pushing and the other two pulling from below. We lost three cameras because we hadn't tied them securely to the raft. It was an expensive lesson. Eventually, we prised the raft free, much to the amusement of the other crew who were watching our efforts from their inflatable in an eddy just below the rapid. But we had the last laugh when, later that day, they hit a half-submerged log. The all leapt for safety as the inflatable raft was sucked underneath the branches. One poor girl, Linda, narrowly missed getting a broken nose when someone accidentally hit her with a paddle.

These were just two incidents on a really exciting trip down the Watut and Markham Rivers. Yet there are so many memories: the clean-swept villages, the *sing sings*, when the men of the village sang with deep bass voices to the rhythm

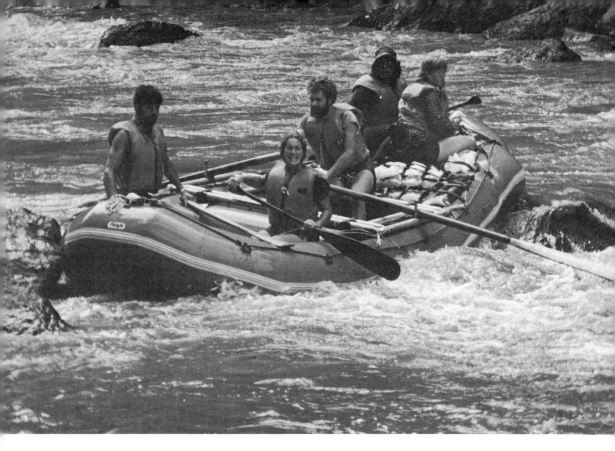

of the drums, which echoed back to us from the side of the valley; and the two tribesmen who dressed up in their ceremonial feathers and beads and gave a war dance with spears.

It's amazing how kind, helpful and generous these people were to us. I'll never forget them. I learned to appreciate the simple life-style of the villagers in Moala and I suppose I learned a great deal about myself too. On an expedition like Operation Drake there's no doubt that you get out of it as much as you put in. In retrospect, I'm sure I could have got more out of it than I did, but that's my fault. Even so, it was one of the most marvellous experiences of my life, one I will never forget.

Nyoli Waghorn visited Europe after Phase 4 had ended and was working in London as a supply nurse when the Eye of the Wind *completed its circumnavigation. She is now working as a nurse in North Island, New Zealand.*

Running the rapids in an Avon inflatable raft on the Watut River, Papua New Guinea. Nyoli Waghorn is at the front, holding a paddle.

PHASE 5   October 1979 – December 1979

Crocodiles, Dragons and Flying Foxes

Stan Glass *United States of America*

It was night on the Strickland River. There were four of us in a small inflatable raft, driven downstream by a 25 h.p. outboard engine. Jerome, in the bows, shone the powerful lamp on some branches snagged on the river bank. Suddenly, he shook the light to attract our attention. He then held it on one spot. Yes . . . there they were: two orange-red discs reflected in the beam. Jerome slowly swung the spotlight across the surface of the black water to show the route of our approach. Bill revved up the engine and sped the raft directly towards the motionless crocodiles. We were tense with excitement. I clung onto the safety-line. 'Wow,' I thought, 'If my friends back in Roosevelt, Long Island could only see me now.'

Stan Glass graduated from Roosevelt High School, New York, in June 1975. He had been at college just over three years and while there had been with fifteen other students to Kenya in East Africa on a Kenya historical tour. It was the first time he had returned to Africa, the home of his forefathers. From then on, he was bitten by the travelling bug.

In 1978, he volunteered for Operation Drake. While he waited for the results of his interview and selection test he sold dictionaries in Long Island to raise some money. Then he received the news he had been waiting for: he was to join the expedition in Papua New Guinea in October 1979.

Papua New Guinea is the second largest island in the world, situated just to the north of Australia and south of the Equator. Many of its animals and plants are unique. Some are spectacular, particularly in the depths of the jungle. In the estuaries of the great rivers, salt-water crocodiles (salties) can grow over 6 metres long while the smaller 4-metre fresh-water crocodiles (freshies) further upriver, are found nowhere else in the world. There are tales of lizards which stand on their hind legs and are over 5 metres long. There are colonies of spiders that spin webs as big as football pitches, spiders that can eat birds, thousands of different insects and vast colonies of bats with wing spans of 1½ metres or more. These are called 'flying foxes'.

Different parts of the country are cut off from each other by mountain ranges over 4,000 metres high. Deep gorges, gulleys and escarpments divide the 3 million people, and there are more than 1,000 tribes speaking over 700 different languages – one quarter of the world's languages. A few tribes were not contacted by white men until the early part of the 1970s and it is rumoured that one or two still remain undetected, hidden in the remoter parts of the tropical rain forest.

Stan was to learn a lot about the rain forest. For 2½ months he and nineteen other members of the expedition travelled by river from north to south across the centre of PNG. They used inflatable boats and dug-out canoes to carry out the first scientific survey of a vast river system which flows through one of the most inaccessible and remote parts of the country.

When we arrived in Nomad, the first 120 kilometres of the upper reaches of the Strickland River were being run by our small white-water team. They had been running rapids in a pair of inflatable rafts for nearly two weeks and were the first people ever to navigate the Strickland Gorge, which is in parts 1,000 metres deep. They planned to be with us in three days' time, when we hoped to have everything ready for the main scientific part of the expedition.

On 10 November, we were to take four inflatable boats and a 14-metre dug-out canoe for a further 800 kilometres down two rivers to the open sea. In our party we had botanists to collect plants, a zoologist to count crocodiles, a herpetologist to collect frogs, lizards and snakes, and an

For over four weeks, members of the expedition motored down the Strickland River in a 14-metre dugout canoe and four inflatables from one scientific camp to another.

anthropologist who, with several interpreters and liaison officers, was to carry out a survey of the people who lived close to the river. Eight different countries were represented on the expedition – Canada, Australia, New Zealand, Britain, Nepal, Fiji, PNG and, of course, dear old USA.

On the afternoon of the third day, just as Pete, Paul, Hosea and I were taking a long cool dip in the river, we heard the 'thwak, thwak' of helicopters approaching. YE's and villagers rushed to the airstrip. It was the eight members of the white-water team, who had been picked up by heli-copter just north of the 'Devil's Race'. It was quite exciting to see those funky, scruffy, 'all-stars', who had already been on the upper reaches of the river for ten days.

Food was prepared to feed thirty-two that evening. The Australian pilots were not leaving until the next morning. It was a great dinner with curried pumpkins, camp pie and crackers, beans and chicken. Real chicken! It was the last we were to taste for the next two months. The next day, at noon, we pushed off from the bank, started up our small outboard engines and waved goodbye. We were off.

It took two days to reach our first camp, which Jim Masters and his small advance party had built on the junction of the Strickland and Nomad Rivers. It was real neat. There were benches and tables, made from bamboo and small jungle trees tied together with twine, for eating and doing scientific work. A huge tarpaulin was stretched over another area. This was where plant and animal specimens could be studied. We had kerosene lamps so that we could work when it was dark. The tarpaulin was really useful because it rained every night, sometimes coming down in torrents.

I was told to join the crocodile team under Jerome Montague, a fellow American, who was working in PNG with the UNDP Crocodile Project. Jerome wanted to conduct the first ever crocodile survey of the Strickland River. We headed up the Strickland in the dug-out canoe. Inside we had everything we needed for the next four days: a deflated rubber raft with another 25 h.p. engine, petrol, food, sleeping gear, emergency flares, a high-powered lamp with a 12-volt battery for spotting crocodiles at night, hand tape-recorders, crocodile counting proformas – the lot.

It took us the whole day, just to reach north of the Cecilia River junction. While we were travelling, Jerome explained what to do and not do when searching for crocs at night. Unlike the Nile crocodiles, which lie up on the banks basking in the sun all day, the PNG freshwater crocodiles can only be seen at night and then only with the aid of a powerful lamp.

Eventually we reached our final campsite on the banks of the Strickland. We unloaded the tents, hammocks and ruck-sacks and got a fire going to cook dinner before dark. Getting things done before nightfall was standard practice. Later on, the fire became our landmark when we returned early in the morning after searching all night for crocodiles.

Everyone in our party, except Rick, Bill and myself, had covered the whole length of the upper reaches of the Strickland River, but no-one had yet spotted any crocodiles. We now wanted to find out if any crocs lived in the brown swirling waters to the north of Cecilia junction. The first night we put the little outboard engine on the back of the raft and motored slowly up river, using the 12-volt battery-

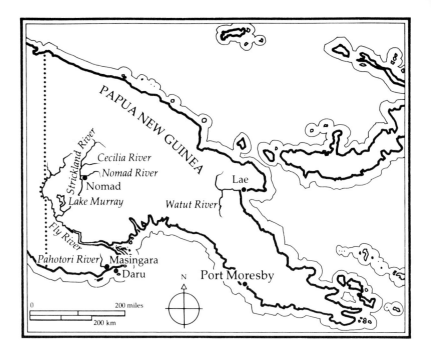

operated lamp to search for logs or any other obstacles float-ing in the water. Just before midnight we turned the raft around, throttled the engine down very low, and used the current to carry us back to our campsite many kilometres downstream. The crocodile search and count was to begin in earnest.

Jerome shone the light from shore to shore. The Strickland was no more than 20–30 metres wide at this point and mov-ing at about 3–4 knots. Left to right, right to left, we strained our eyes looking for those two orange-red discs – the eyes of a crocodile.

Then we saw one. Bill pointed the raft straight at it. Wakker got his camera out and tried to film as I picked up the crocodile reports and my torch, ready to jot down notes about the crocodile as Jerome shouted them out to me. I also tried to dip one of the paddles into the river to check the depth of the water. There was a lot to do. Everybody was excited and busy. The raft was the only thing between us and the crocodiles. Boy, did I love that little rubber raft!

We drew closer to the crocodile. It lay half in the water and half out, but far enough out for us to see that it was a fresh-water, and not a salt-water crocodile. You can tell this from the bumps at the back of its neck and because it's much darker in colour than the 'salty'. I had to record what size it was, what time we had seen it, where it was found and what reactions it had had as we approached it. The fact that we had got so close showed that the crocodiles up here had not been hunted before. At last, we had seen our first crocodile in the wild.

On we motored, back to the deeper part of the river, and shone the light again from shore to shore, left to right, right to left. Then a waving light, two red discs, revving the engines and moving in. We did this about twenty-five times that first night. As we continued down the river over the next month, moving from campsite to campsite, we counted over 840 crocodiles.

Jerome was very happy with the results of our survey. Everything had gone as he had hoped. The first survey of the Strickland River had been completed and all the results had been submitted to the United Nations Crocodile Project. The statistics were important to this part of PNG because so many crocodiles on the lower reaches of the river had been shot by hunters that there were fewer and fewer skins to sell on the world market. Crocodile skins are an important part of PNG's economy.

Five different scientific camps were set up by Jim Masters and his small advance group along the Strickland. They normally set off a couple of days before the main body to give themselves enough time to build it. Around these camps, there was plenty to interest the scientists. Jim Croft and Hosea Gideon collected over 500 species of plants for the Division of Botany in Lae and made a random survey of the types of vegetation along the banks of both the Strickland and Fly Rivers. Often I used to trek with them in the bush, all of us wearing yellow helmets to protect us from the branches which were shot off upper parts of selected trees with Jim's old shotgun. It seemed a crazy way to collect plants to me, but it worked.

Rupert Gray and his small team had an interesting job contacting tribesmen in their small villages or hunting camps along the river. We had been asked by the PNG government to ask the villagers a variety of questions to help find out more about them and the way they live. We managed to understand each other, thanks to Uge, our Moto-speaking interpreter.

Ian Redmond spent most of each night searching for frogs and snakes with a headtorch. He used to record frog croaks on his small tape-recorder, then play them back to another unsuspecting frog. This often resulted in quite a heated interchange between the two of them before Ian crept up and captured the live one. One specimen jumped into Roger

Ian Redmond, zoologist, with one of the snakes he collected on the Strickland River.

Kurt Foelmer (Canada)
helps zoologist Ian
Redmond to catalogue
and label frogs and lizards
as they move down the
Strickland River.

Chapman's cup of tea – I heard later that it had previously
been unknown to science.

Evenings on the river were magnificent. After supper we
often used to sit alongside the boats and stare at the broad
river and red sunset and watch the great flocks of flying
foxes flapping their way down river to their feeding
grounds. There were literally thousands of them. Some
would dive out of the sky and swoop straight down towards
us then glide away just above our heads.

On the lower reaches, close to Lake Murray, we were often
visited by the local tribespeople in their long dug-out
canoes. They stood in their canoes and dipped the circular
blades of their paddles into the water to propel themselves
along. Some would come to the campsite with small
crocodiles for Jerome and Ian to look at.

Eventually, on 9 December, the whole team arrived at
Daru, just beyond the estuary of the Fly River, for a rendezvous with the *Eye of the Wind*. Carefully our team winched
aboard the inflatable rafts and all the equipment. On deck,
the skipper welcomed each of us with an ice-cold beer. It

was the best reward we could have had after five weeks on the river. What a great welcome.

Sadly, Ian Redmond and I had to clamber back over the rail, down to the long-boat bobbing alongside and wave goodbye to the rest of the team as they set sail and moved slowly out to sea. We had been detailed to join the 'great lizard hunt' at Masingara just up the coast from Daru, while the *Eye of the Wind* returned to Port Moresby.

There had been many reports of dragons in south-west Papua New Guinea. As recently as 1952, an Australian animal ecologist had investigated these strange stories and come to the conclusion that the long tailed 'dragon' which stood on its hind legs was a giant lizard – the Salvador Monitor. Some had been captured which were 3 metres long, although it was thought that the monitor could grow to a length of well over 5 metres.

When I joined the twenty-strong team in the beautiful village of Masingara, with its traditional stilt-supported bamboo huts, the team was busily questioning the villagers. One white-haired old lady had told John Blashford-Snell, the

Spectators watch the arrival of the Eye of the Wind *at the small island of Daru at the mouth of the Fly River, PNG.*

leader of the giant lizard hunt, that hunters from the village had often come across these creatures. In fact, she said, they were quite common, but the villagers treated them with great respect. Apparently, a captured monitor lizard had once smashed its way out of a stout cage and killed a large guard dog with its powerful claws before escaping back into the forest.

Before we divided into four small patrols and went out into the jungle, we were shown photographs of our quarry. About two-thirds of the lizard consists of its tail which is dragged behind its body by four stubby powerful legs. We learned that the lizard's method of hunting is to lie in wait on the lower branches of trees before dropping onto its victim and tearing it apart.

The jungle was much more swampy than anything we had experienced up the Fly and Strickland Rivers and very hard going. The mosquitoes were hell. Whenever we met local hunters we drew diagrams of the lizard in the earth with a stick. They seemed to understand what we wanted and pointed deeper into the jungle. Sometimes we would rest near likely hunting grounds and keep watch for hours on end, but we didn't see a thing. Many times we laid up over night at waterholes, looking and listening.

Caroline Buxton (Jersey) lies alongside a small 3.25-metre Salvador monitor lizard. It is said that these lizards can grow to a length of more than 5 metres.

As we were motoring back from one hunting trip down the Pahotori River, news came over the radio that a local hunter had shot a big monitor and was returning to Masingara with it. We returned to the village at full speed. When we arrived at the village, a large crowd had gathered in a circle around the lizard which was on the ground stretched out and roped to a bamboo pole. It was very dead, but still looked quite fearsome. Ian Redmond cut it open and examined it in detail before he announced that it was a baby monitor lizard, about 2½ metres long. We wondered what a grown adult would look like!

Time was running short for the YE's; our phase was rapidly coming to an end. Unfortunately, we had to return to Port Moresby to pack up our belongings and souvenirs such as bows and arrows, shell necklaces and carved bamboo smoking pipes which we had been given by the kind people we had met during our patrols through PNG. Three months had gone in a flash.

Although I've mentioned only two of the ten or so projects on Phase 5 of Operation Drake, I know that every other YE's adventures were just as exciting as mine. Whether they were diving off the east coast of PNG looking for sunken vessels, aircraft and charting underwater wrecks; helping scientists with the many projects around base camp and up the aerial walkway; discovering coal shales on Cape Finisterre; locating crashed aircraft in the mountains; exploring Japanese wartime bunkers; carrying out medical projects amongst primitive peoples; collecting medicinal plants on the islands off the east coast of PNG, I could go on and on . . . they were all equally fascinating. It had been a great experience.

Stan Glass returned to New York to complete his studies in insurance. In 1980, he travelled to London to see the return of the Eye of the Wind *and introduce his father to the many friends he made on Operation Drake.*

PHASE 6   December 1979 – February 1980

Jungle Camps and Gentle People

Sue Mattson *Australia*

We were taught how to catch monkeys, birds, fish and even crocodiles. Our newly-gained knowledge soon came in useful when, at the end of our six-day survival course in Sulawesi, we were dumped on a small island by ourselves for two days, without any food. On the first night my palm leaf shelter collapsed in a tropical downpour and I was bitten all over by mosquitoes. I spent all the next day standing up to my neck in the sea to avoid the sun and those horrible creepy crawlies. I only came out to look for shellfish to eat. It was a marvellous way to diet, I can tell you.

Sue Mattson was twenty-two years old when she heard she had been selected for Operation Drake. After leaving school she had worked on her father's fishing boat along the south coast of Australia, hunting for sharks and trawling for sea salmon. It was hard work but gave her a healthy respect for the sea. This came in very useful when, with twenty-three other YE's, she joined the Eye of the Wind *at Port Moresby in Papua New Guinea on Phase 6 of Operation Drake.*

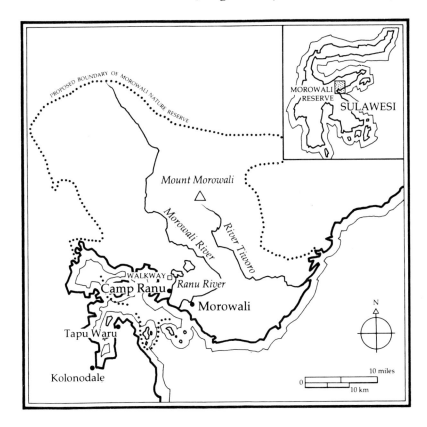

When the YE's arrived in PNG most of the staff were packing for the move to Sulawesi in Indonesia. In Francis Drake's time Indonesia was known as 'the Spice Islands' or 'the Celebes', and Sulawesi is the largest of the five main islands. The name Indonesia is made up of two Greek words, 'indo', meaning East Indian, and 'nesos' meaning islands. Thus, Sulawesi is one of 6,000 or so 'East Indian' islands.

All the YE's had a marvellous, carefree approach to the voyage. The azure-blue waters and clear skies put everyone in a happy-go-lucky mood; there was lots of laughing and joking as the *Eye of the Wind* glided through the calm seas towards Sulawesi. We thought that the whole voyage would be one long, relaxed holiday. Then the squalls hit us. Suddenly, seas crashed over our bows as we plunged deep into the green troughs of the waves and keeled over under the lash of the winds. The force of the gale was fantastic and we were ordered up the rigging to haul in the top sails*. Many of the YE's were terribly seasick, but somehow they forced themselves to go on, although they must have felt like death. At times, we had to have all hands on deck.

After the excitement of the storm at sea, I will never forget the bliss of sailing into the graceful bay leading to Kolondale, on the east coast of Sulawesi. Canoes came out to meet us, crammed with golden-brown islanders dressed in colourful sarongs. They all waved and smiled. When we eventually berthed at the jetty, hundreds of people came out to greet us. It was unforgettable. After all the jobs were done I looked over the side of the ship and saw a green wall of jungle stretching up towards the blue mountains beyond. It was so beautiful; it was like Paradise.

Sulawesi is one of the biggest islands of Indonesia covering an area of some 227,000 square kilometres. It is a curious shape being about 1,200 kilometres long with a coastline of approximately 3,000 kilometres. Its width varies from 30 to 200 kilometres. The coast is fringed by coral reefs with many shoals and banks. In the interior, the island is very mountainous, and is mostly covered by lush jungle. Although it has a hot climate, it is cooled by strong sea winds. It is a real tropical rain forest island.

It took us two hours to travel by boat to reach Camp Ranu. Sometimes we stopped to push our long boats over half-

An aerial view of the base camp on Ranu River in Sulawesi. It consisted of sleeping huts, a cookhouse, a medical centre, a survey centre, signal huts and laboratories. It housed up to 141 scientists, administrators and Young Explorers who were conducting a survey of the Morowali Nature Reserve.

submerged logs and branches. I couldn't see any animals. Apart from the occasional grunts and squawks from the jungle, everything was silent and mysterious. We didn't even see any crocodiles, which are supposed to live on the banks of the dark brown river. Occasionally, we were caught by overhanging branches and lianas with short sharp thorns which tore our clothes and skin. We continued up the Ranu River for what seemed like ages until, suddenly, we saw a small jetty made of logs. It was Camp Ranu: a series of long-houses, built on stilts by our small advance party, in a clearing in the jungle.

Operation Drake was to work from Camp Ranu for six months to help the World Wildlife Fund make the vast area of land to the east of the gulf of Morowali into a nature reserve. In order to do this a very full report had to be written to prove to the Indonesian Government how important it was to conserve this 2,000 square-kilometre area as a wildlife sanctuary. The YE's were to help scientists conduct the research necessary for the report. It all sounded very exciting.

A few of the longhouses were not quite complete and were roofed with plastic sheets; but the majority were covered with jungle leaves lashed together to keep out the rain. The floors of the longhouses were built off the ground so that snakes, termites or ants couldn't get in. We slung our hammocks from the roof and draped them with mosquito nets so that bugs couldn't bite us in the night. It was so humid that even this quite simple job made us hot and sweaty.

Camp Ranu soon became our home. We got to know the staff and the scientists and settled down into a daily routine. Every morning I got up at 6 a.m. and walked down to the river to wash. It was lovely dipping into the cool, clear water, before drying and making my way up to the kitchen hut with a canvas bucket of water. Breakfast consisted of muesli, dried biscuits and jam, followed by tea or coffee. That was quite enough in this heat and humidity.

After breakfast we were split up and allocated to different scientists to work as their assistants for the day. Most of the scientists had been out in the area for several weeks before we arrived and were already deeply involved in their scientific programmes and researches in the jungle. I worked with Andrew Lack who was trying to find out which plants grew in the area. Every day we would observe the insects on certain bushes and plants. This meant standing for hours on end counting different types of insects and recording which type visited which flower. We were trying to work out how the plants were pollinated.

Some YE's went out with the medical teams into remote villages to carry out blood sampling tests among the local people, whilst others observed bird life, or caught bats, insects, snakes and butterflies. As a result of this research we hoped to compile a complete picture of the area.

In the late afternoon, when we returned from the day's work, we usually swam in the river to cool off before assembling in the kitchen hut for supper. Dave, our cook, would make a delicious meal out of dried vegetables and whatever meat and fish we had in the camp at the time. After supper we sat at the tables, wrote up our notes and discussed various points for the report. This was also the ideal time to fill in our diaries. The rest of the evening was spent chatting about our different countries and then having a sing-song around the camp fire. We were always very tired by the time we collapsed into out hammocks. Even the noises of the jungle – the piping of frogs, the screech of night birds and the ring of the cicada – couldn't keep us awake.

One of my first projects was to help build an aerial walkway so that the scientists could observe the animal and plant life 40 metres up in the canopy of the rain forest. The walkway consisted of narrow metal ladders joined together to form a platform. It was suspended from the tree tops by man-made fibre tapes and went off in various directions into the canopy. It must have been over 100 metres long.

We reached the top by climbing a rope ladder. This was the worst part for me because it swung wildly and I had to force myself not to look down. In fact, once you are so far up, you can't see the small faces below because the lower branches of the trees get in the way. We had to wear a safety harness the whole time. Even so, we worked our way along the walkway with extreme care and held onto the webbing handrails very firmly indeed. But it didn't take us long to feel completely at home in the canopy of the jungle, and the wildlife was fascinating.

To get down, we had to abseil down a rope suspended from one of the tallest trees using a karabiner harness. This is quite safe, and a common way of getting down mountains, but one day I was suddenly stopped half-way down and almost throttled by my camera strap which had caught round an overhanging branch. I hung there, looking very undignified, until someone at last abseiled down alongside me and set me free.

John Rimmer (England), suspended 40 metres above the ground in the rain forest canopy, puts the finishing touches to the aerial walkway. This walkway enabled scientists to observe and collect specimens in the canopy. Operation Drake built similar walkways in Panama, Papua New Guinea and Sulawesi and were the first to use this method of studying the tropical rain forest. Over 80% of the insects collected were new to science.

This was the third time a walkway had been used on Operation Drake, and it allowed the scientists to make a comparative study of the tropical rain forests of Panama, PNG and Indonesia. When the walkway was finished, Andrew and I used to climb up it every day to observe the flowers in the jungle canopy. Often we took nectar samples from them. It was also possible to see how the pollen was passed from flower to flower, so enabling them to germinate. It was a breathtaking experience to lean out from the walkway. I had to concentrate on the job in hand rather than think about the 40-metre drop below me. Even now, I shudder when I remember what we had to do.

On 25 January we were split into two groups and sent to separate Indonesian villages for seven days. Our aim was to

The Young Explorers took part in all the day-to-day activities of village life. They had to work for their food, either harvesting rice or crops in the fields, or fishing at sea from dug-out canoes.

live like the villagers and, in so doing, to study their way of life. In this way, it was felt that we would appreciate how the local people used the forest and the sea to survive. It would also help us see how the environment affected people's way of life in a developing country.

I was sent to Tapu-Waru on the coast. This was a small village of farmers and fishermen. I was welcomed into the home of a delightful lady called Nee-ha. As only one member of our team could speak Indonesian and none of the villagers could speak English, we had to start learning their language from scratch. We used to sit in Nee-ha's hut and exchange simple words. We shrieked with laughter at each other's attempts to pronounce words in a strange tongue. Nee-ha found English a very amusing language.

The villagers were a very lovely and gentle people, always laughing and joking. They seemed to be very happy. They were very curious about us – especially the children. They used to follow us everywhere, never leaving us alone. They were always offering us food and sometimes they invited us to share delicious meals of rice, fish and vegetables. We couldn't refuse, even if we weren't hungry, because they would have been hurt.

While we were in Tapu-Waru we worked all day in the fields and went out fishing at night with lamps to attract the fish. Hilary, the other girl in our group, and I went fishing after much discussion with two of Nee-ha's sons. They thought it most unusual that two girls should want to do such a thing. In Indonesia only the men go out fishing; the women stay at home or work in the fields. Nee-ha was rather anxious about us and even took a canoe out herself to make sure that we were alright. She was like a second mother to us. Fishing was fun. The two men hung a lamp on the bow of the canoe to attract the fish, then threw the nets over the side. When the nets were heavy we helped to land them and pull the fish out of the nets. We brought in lots of different types of fish. Nee-ha was delighted.

Another day we went planting rice with the family in a clearing on a steep mountainside. We tried very hard to copy our hosts, but were not very good. Much to the amusement of the villagers, we kept falling over as we bent down to plant the rice or got wedged in between the logs left over from the burning of the forest.

Sue Mattson washes her clothes, watched by amused villagers in Tapu Waru, Sulawesi.

We also climbed up a mountain to where the felled logs lay. One of them had been carved into a dug-out canoe by several of the village elders. Our job was to get the canoe down the mountain and to launch it in the sea. There were about thirty men with us, who hauled at the canoe with ropes and tackle and pulled it over a series of logs laid in the bed of a dried-up creek. It crashed and banged along the logs until suddenly it shot out of control down the mountainside with all of us chasing after it, shouting and cheering. We had a great feast after the canoe was successfully launched.

There was only one thing I found difficult to do in this close-knit little community – having a swim. The women wear beautiful sarongs even when swimming so when I wore my bikini I almost caused an uproar. As a result, I had to copy the Indonesian women – and, as you can imagine, it's mighty difficult changing out of a wet sarong into a dry one when most of the village is watching you!

During the last week of my stay in Sulawesi, I travelled with a survey team on a six-day journey to one of the more remote areas in the Morowali district. We stayed in a small village called Kaipdi, the home of the Wana people. The village had only four longhouses, built several metres apart, at the base of the mountains from which the Morawali River flows.

The 'wild' Wana, a tribe found to the north of the Solato

River, are feared by all other tribes. The literal translation of their name *Kayu Merangka* is 'blowing leaves'. They are called this because every time someone in authority comes near them or tries to approach them, they disappear like the 'blowing leaves of the night'. They are said to be fierce and to have attacked other settlements.

In fact, we found the Wana tribe a peaceful people who jealously guarded their isolation from the outside world. The men still went out hunting with blow pipes and poisonous darts. When they were not hunting, some collected *damar*, a sap collected from the trunks of certain trees which is made into glass. Bags of *damar* can weigh up to 40 kilogrammes. These tough, wiry people run long distances across rugged country, with the bags over their shoulders, to reach the market. Their stamina and strength is amazing. We felt very honoured to be allowed to stay with them during the survey.

Time passed far too quickly. In mid-March I had to say farewell to all the many friends I had made, with whom I had been through so much. I think it was that which linked us so closely together. I didn't want to leave Sulawesi with its rugged, yet beautiful countryside and its peaceful and gentle people. Nor did I want to leave Operation Drake and return to Australia, but my three-month phase was over. I had to make way for the other YE's who were lucky enough to be able to visit this part of the tropical world.

Sue Mattson returned to Australia to help her father fish for shark and salmon, though she is saving to head overseas once more. As she says, 'Operation Drake broadened my outlook on life to such an extent that I want to make the most of it before my time is up!'

Above *River-running in an Avon 'Professional' inflatable raft down the Watut River in Papua New Guinea.*

Left *Noel English holds up a 'flying fox' bat which he captured in a wire bat trap in Sulawesi, Indonesia. Flying foxes have wingspans of up to 1½ metres.*

On arriving in Papua New Guinea, every young explorer attended a five-day jungle acquaintance course, which included long route marches through the rain forest.

Above right *This three-toed sloth and her baby were rescued by young explorers from their treetop home during a forest clearance scheme. Later the sloths were released into one of Panama's nature reserves.*

Above *Claire Bertschinger, nurse, makes a friend of a baby green parrot close to Caledonia Bay, Panama.*

Young explorers drag fresh supplies to the walkway camp 5 kilometres up the Ranu River in Sulawesi, Indonesia.

PHASE 7   February 1980 – April 1980

Drake's Cannons and Other Assortments

Conway Leung Nim-ho *Hongkong*

After living in the concrete jungle of Hongkong for more than twenty years, I wanted to get away from people and taste adventure. A chance to get into the real jungle seemed too good to miss.

Conway Leung Nim-ho was a police sergeant with the Royal Hongkong Police Force when the chance came to go on Phase 7 of Operation Drake. He was well fitted for the expedition, being a canoeing instructor, a qualified parachutist, an advanced rock-climber and – what would prove to be particularly useful in Sulawesi – a deep-sea diver. He had had some experience of living in the jungle on an outward bound course in the New Territories of Hongkong, but he had long wanted to familiarise himself with it further. Seven days after leaving Hongkong he could hardly believe he was in Camp Ranu preparing to lead a small foot patrol deep into the tropical rain forest of Sulawesi to the deserted village of Scolare. The local people called it 'the lost village'.

One of the jobs the YE's had to do was to make contact with as many of the local tribes as possible and tell them of the plan to make the 2,000 square-kilometre area of Morowali into a nature reserve. It was important to discover if the once deserted village of Scolare had been reoccupied. If it had, it could be marked on the large-scale map the survey team had drawn up for the Indonesian government.

One of the directing staff gave me a map showing a possible route to the village of Scolare. He told our patrol to find the village, discover if anyone lived there and then report back. A Gurkha soldier was to accompany us and he would operate the radio so that we could keep in contact with base camp. We were given enough food for a week and survival rations. This was just the sort of independence we wanted. It was up to us to do the job without help.

With great confidence we shouldered our heavy rucksacks, waved goodbye to those who were staying at Camp Ranu and set off at a cracking pace into the jungle. In single file we started to follow a small hunting track through the dense foliage. But the track became less distinct the further we travelled and the undergrowth became darker, wetter and more tangled. It was very hot and humid. We crossed countless gullies and small streams and once, as we clambered up a small hill, we had to crawl.

Every few minutes I checked the route on the map, though it didn't seem to relate to the ground. Many streams were unmarked and the track often divided, making it hard to decide which way to go. I tried to count my steps and work out how far we had gone, but it was hopeless. After a couple of hours I was completely lost. There was only one thing for it: we would have to cut our way out of the jungle to the main river on a compass bearing. We hacked and hacked at the thick foliage with our machetes, taking it in turns to take the lead. But even so our progress seemed painfully slow. To add to our misery, it rained. At last, however, we emerged just before darkness fell. And, as luck would have it, there was a small village close by.

We stayed in the village overnight and the next morning I managed to employ a guide. He said that he knew Scolare and could find it easily. So, with our guide in front, we re-entered the forest feeling a little more confident. Not long afterwards we came to Kayu Poli, a small farming village

where we bought some greens to supplement our rations. Then we pressed on to the River Pampongo. The going was much easier than the day before.

That afternoon, as we were walking along a track by the river, we came face to face with a group of Wana people. They were dark-skinned, short and naked, apart from a sarong around the waist. The group was a small hunting party, armed with 3-metre-long bamboo blow-pipes. Each man carried a large cylinder-like quiver, full of poisonous darts. When a hunter sees a game bird in the branches of a tree he carefully selects a 30-centimetre-long dart, wraps some kapok around its base and pushes it up the blow-pipe until it is wedged. With great accuracy, he points it at the bird – which can be as far as 40 metres away – takes a large breath, and blows. 'Phut!' The sliver of bamboo travels faster than the eye can see. The dead bird tumbles out of the tree onto the ground.

It turned out that one of the party had met some YE's a short time before, and he explained to the other tribesmen what we were doing. He became quite chatty and told us that the Wana not only hunt but also collect *damar* for making glazes for pottery and *rattan*, a cane used for making furniture. The cane is cut down in the forest with *parangs* – very sharp, long-bladed knives similar to our machetes – which they all carry in bamboo sheaths hung from their shoulders. Because everything grows so quickly in the jungle, this destruction doesn't really harm the environment, but the Wana's custom of burning down large patches of jungle to plant their crops in the ashes is more destructive. After a couple of years, the torrential rains have washed away the surface soil from the clearing, so making the area infertile. By then the Wana have moved on.

Next day we climbed a ridge of Mount Morowali, following the supposed route to the 'lost' village. Despite all we had heard about snakes, spiders and ferocious wild animals in the jungle, the only interesting creatures we saw were some lizards about 2 metres long. With beady eyes, they watched us from the undergrowth, flicking their forked tongues, then slowly lumbered back into the undergrowth. They appeared far less afraid of us then we were of them.

At length we reached Scolare, which had been abandoned twenty years before by its inhabitants, who had gone to seek a better life on the coast. It was still deserted. The huts on stilts were rotting with age and creepers grew up their bamboo walls. Some of the roofs had caved in and one hut had collapsed completely. It was rather eerie walking through those silent, skeleton-like structures which once housed a whole village. The small plantation alongside the village was completely covered in weeds. Elsewhere saplings, ferns and bushes grew freely. It was obvious that in a few years' time Scolare would completely disappear. We drew a small sketch map, took measurements, made notes and then began our slow and steady return to Camp Ranu, our first task successfully completed.

Our second task was to search for Drake's cannons. At the start of her voyage, the *Golden Hind* was carrying eighteen cannons and hundreds of cannon balls, each weighing about 4 kilogrammes. The cannon balls were not large enough to sink an enemy ship but, with accurate gunnery, could tear holes in its sails and bring down its mast. More damage was done by the swivel guns which were mounted on the poop of the *Golden Hind* to send shot showering across the deck of the enemy vessel.

By 1580 the *Golden Hind* was on a westerly course bound for home, with a hold full of Spanish treasure and precious spices. But on the evening of 9 January she sailed into a storm and ran aground on a submerged and uncharted coral reef, now known as Vesuvius reef. The crew was convinced she would sink; the ship's chaplain blamed the disaster on Drake's sinful past. What was certain was that the ship was stuck fast and, as night fell, it became obvious that there was little hope of moving her. In desperation, Drake ordered eight of the eighteen cannons to be trundled overboard in an attempt to lighten the ship and so free her from the coral reef. The attempt failed. Next, half the precious cargo of cloves was dumped into the lashing waves. But still nothing happened; the *Golden Hind* remained firmly aground. But then, just as the ship juddered and began to keel over, a fierce gust of wind jerked her free from the reef. By a tremendous piece of luck she had not been holed, so she was able to sail away and continue her journey towards home. The eight cannons were left behind.

Our first dive was to secure brightly coloured buoys to the side of the reef to act as markers for the aeroplane which was to sweep the area with a metal detector in an attempt to locate the cannons. I adjusted my mask and breathing apparatus, then jumped over the side clutching one of the buoy's long ropes in my right hand. Slowly I descended the cliff-like sides of the reef, looking for a suitable anchor point for the rope on the sharp coral. At last, I found one and threaded the loose end through a hole and tied it secure. The bubbles from my air cylinder rose to the shimmering surface of the sea 10 metres above. There was no sound apart from my steady breathing and the regular release of air from the tank. It was only after I'd secured my first buoy and was about to kick myself away from the side of the reef that I noticed the incredible beauty of the coral.

The sides of the reef plunged down for hundreds of metres, but in such water it was possible to see every detail

Robbie Williamson (England) instructs Young Explorers in Tomori Bay in the use of scuba equipment. This was to prepare them for marine survey work and the search for Francis Drake's cannon on Vesuvius Reef.

Roger Bacon (England), standing, Peter Lau (Hong Kong) and Conway Leung Nim-ho look on as two Young Explorers continue the search for the rare and elusive dugong on Vesuvius Reef.

of the coral. Dappled bluish-green light flickered over the jagged and pock-marked surface of the hundreds of different types of coral; the swaying weeds and plants which clung to its surface waved in my face. As I hung motionless in the water, multi-coloured striped fish darted out of the weeds as if fascinated by my mask; they seemed mesmerised by the escaping bubbles of air. There was so much activity on the reef, I felt I could have stayed there for ever amid the vivid, unreal colours – but, I had a job of work to do.

We dived four times, placing markers in different positions along the edge of the reef. Each dive was equally enchanting. At times I felt I could have dived to the bottom of the ocean because it looked so clear and tempting, but I knew that I had to keep checking my depth gauge strapped to my wrist. If you go deeper than 10 metres the pressure of the water produces a sharp pain in your ears, and if you ascend too quickly from a deep dive you can get the 'bends'. These are cramps which are so severe they can kill you. On one occasion I foolishly dived too quickly and the rapid build-up of pressure caused my nose to bleed. It gave me quite a scare because on the previous dive we'd noticed a couple of sharks cruising along the edge of the reef. Obviously, my blood wasn't very attractive, or I probably wouldn't be here to tell the tale!

Two days later, at about 10 o'clock, we heard the sound of
an aircraft engine and then saw the Royal Australian Air
force *Orion* approaching low over the water. For two hours
the aircraft made sweeps over the 10-square-kilometre reef.
now clearly marked by the orange buoys bobbing in the
light blue water. The reef is almost circular in shape, its flat
top slightly dipping in the centre, partially covered in thick
sea grass. At high water the coral is about a metre below the
surface and at low water the outer rim of the reef is just
visible above the waves. At midday the aircraft obviously
located something. It circled, then dropped a smoke flare
close to the edge of the reef. Could this be what we had come
so far to find?

The diving team jumped aboard the inflatable raft and
motored across to the burning flare. One by one the divers
tumbled backwards into the glassy waters. Slowly we
searched. At last, we found a pile of scrap metal, obviously
dumped by a ship which had run aground many years
before. Of the eight cannons, there was no sign. The aircraft
continued for another hour until at 1.30 p.m. the pilot told us
he would have to return to base. No other metal had been
detected. As he left he dropped a parachute into the sea with
a waterproof container full of newspapers, fruit juice and
fresh milk. It was a kind and thoughtful gesture.

During the next five days we continued diving with
snorkels over the whole surface of the reef to complete a
marine biological survey report. We recorded a wealth of
marine life, including information on turtles and the rare
dugong (sea-cow). Legend has it that sailors were often
lured to their deaths by mermaids who lay on rocks combing
their long hair and singing to the sailors, thereby enticing

*The search for Drake's
cannon was helped by
the use of a metal
detector. The magnetic
readings led the divers to
investigate stacks of
rusty metal which had
been dumped by more
modern ships which had
run aground on the
uncharted reef. The
cannon were not
located.*

them to steer their ships onto the rocks. Today, many scientists think that these mermaids were in fact dugongs, although it strikes me that the sailors must have been at sea a very long time indeed to make such a mistake and to find anything attractive about the sack-like, bloated, be-whiskered sea-cow! However, Trish Holdway was very excited by the number of dugongs we found amidst the sea grass in the centre of the reef and submitted a report to the Indonesian government suggesting that the whole of Vesuvius reef be made into a marine nature reserve.

Obviously we were disappointed not to find the cannons because that was the main reason we'd sailed to Vesuvius reef. But, as a direct result of our marine survey, the government declared it a 'protected area'. In future no ship would be allowed to approach it or anchor off it; no ship would be able to empty its oil tanks and contaminate this uniquely beautiful stretch of reef; and the dugong would be able to breed and bask undisturbed amidst the coral and sea grass.

This was not the only good news. The combined efforts of Phases 6 and 7 to produce a management report for the proposed Morowali nature reserve also bore fruit. When the *Eye of the Wind* eventually returned to Jakarta, the capital of Indonesia, the Indonesian Director-General of Forestry addressed us with these words: 'Morowali will now be safeguarded for the future as part of the national heritage which will be passed on to future generations of Indonesians. It is one thing which you, the scientists and Young Explorers of Operation Drake, can really take a pride in having helped to create. I thank you on behalf of the government of Indonesia for all you have done and I wish you and the *Eye of the Wind* bon voyage and the very best for the future.'

Without doubt, Operation Drake has been the biggest event in my life. It has broadened my horizons and helped me acquire much more self-confidence. I think it has also helped me to develop qualities of leadership, because a short time after I returned to duty with the Hongkong Police Force I was promoted to Inspector. Above all, I have learned to get on with people from many different countries and backgrounds. This is bound to stand me in good stead in my job as a policeman in such a cosmopolitan city as Hongkong.

Conway Leung Nim-ho is working in the Hongkong Police Force, though he is still interested in teaching young people scuba-diving and other adventurous pursuits.

PHASE 8   April 1980 – June 1980

Coral Reefs and Wild-life Safaris

Diane Burroughes *Canada*

My legs were shaking as I moved slowly along the swaying footropes suspended from the top gallant* yard*. My nerves took over and I trembled violently. If you're tall you can bend over the yard at the waist to get a feeling of security, but I was too small for that. To get control of myself, I looked far out to sea. I gripped the jackstay* so tight you'd have needed pliers to prise my fingers away. Rock climbing was never this hairy!

Diane Burroughes was brought up on a beef farm north of Toronto in Ontario. She was twenty-four years old when she was selected for Operation Drake and had already been to university and completed her teacher training course. In just two days she found herself transported from the familiar surroundings of Canada to Jakarta in Indonesia. It was very strange to be in a tropical city on the other side of the world, but not as extraordinary as those first eight days at sea. Diane had never been to sea before she joined Phase 8 of Operation Drake.

The *Eye of the Wind* conjures up a romantic image in most people's minds, but not in mine. I just think of all those sailing words and seventy-five different pin positions to be learned by heart – when to pull the downhaul* or halyard*, slacken the sheets*, the clewlines* and buntlines* for fifteen different sails! Fortunately, none of the other twenty-one YE's had much sailing experience either. How funny it must have been to watch us stagger along the plunging deck, trying to grab hold of something to steady ourselves, instead of just swaying with the swells as the ship rolled.

The trade winds left us as we took in the sails in the sheltered lee of Direction Island, one of the Cocos (Keeling) Islands, on 22 May 1980. It was my first sight of a tropical island: swaying palms, long white beaches and a marvellous turquoise-green lagoon. To me, it was one of the wonders of the world.

The Cocos (Keeling) Islands consist of two atolls [circular coral reefs enclosing a lagoon]. The southern atoll is the only inhabited part of Cocos (Keeling). Both have many sea birds and turtles, as well as giant robber-crabs which eat coconuts which have fallen from the palms along the white beaches. The islands were discovered in 1609 by a British sea captain, William Keeling, but they were not inhabited until 1823, when an Englishman settled on one of the atolls. Later, in 1927, John Clunies-Ross, a Shetland islander, and his family settled on the other island and started to cultivate the wild coconut palms. In 1955, the islands were handed over to the Australians and the Ross family moved to Home Island, where they still live today.

The island's council had asked us to help with a number of community projects. We started by demolishing an old copra drying shed and helping to build a meeting house for the council. We knocked down cement walls, dug ditches and, eventually, when most of the rubble had been cleared away, used our tractor to rip out an old tin shed. It was hard work, and hot. Hard, because we were using our arm muscles for the first time, and hot because the other girls and I had to wear trousers out of respect to those islanders who were Muslim. While we worked, we could see and hear the Malay women cracking open coconuts so that the white flesh could be dried in huge ovens or in the sun. The dried coconut flesh, which is known as copra, is exported and processed to extract its valuable natural oils. The husks of the coconuts are treated separately; the fibrous hair is used to make rope and matting.

We left the Cocos (Keeling) Islands to sail across the Indian Ocean. It was to be a 4,000 kilometre journey taking eighteen days. To prepare us for storms and possible sightings of dolphins, sharks, whales and flying fish, the watch-keepers organised a series of explanatory lectures. Lecture times were posted on the blackboard in the galley. We learned about navigation, the weather, the sea, marine-biology, sail handling and knots. If you were interested enough, you could learn about the history of the brigantines, the development of square-rigged sailing ships, celestial navigation, and how to use a sextant*. But surprisingly, there was always so much to do on board, it was difficult to find time to attend as many lectures as we would have liked.

Everyone had a turn at the helm*, but after a couple of hours you began to see double numbers on the compass in front of you and had to keep shaking your head to keep alert. On night watch, if you were lucky, you might see a school of dolphins glide effortlessly under the bow. The stars were so large and bright you could almost pluck them from the sky. You swore you could see their reflections on the dark surface of the sea, until a dolphin streaked across the waters. Suddenly, you realised that those reflections were phosphorescent creatures, glowing like fireflies.

On the bosun's watch, which was the day maintenance watch, there was an immense amount of work to do: continuous chipping, painting, sanding-down of the wood to re-varnish it, splicing* and whipping* ropes. All hard work, but fun.

Galley watch was really tough. From 6.30 a.m. until 8.30 p.m. you served meals and washed up. 'How would you like your egg this morning, fried, scrambled or poached?' You peeled potatoes, cut up onions, and crushed garlic cloves on the deck. Cleaning the heads (lavatories) and scrubbing the galley floor were other daily jobs.

On the morning of the eighteenth day, I woke up early and went on deck. I saw Mahe, one of the Seychelles Islands, approaching fast. Quickly I went below, put on my shoes and went forward to stand on 'lookout' with Monica, as we sailed into Port Victoria.

The Seychelles consist of some ninety-two islands. They are home for about 62,000 people. A few of these are descendants of African slaves and English sailors, others are deportees from France and some are Chinese or Indian. Most are Roman Catholic although there are tales of witchcraft on the islands. They speak English, French or a sort of Creole patois.

There are very few animals on the islands apart from rats and bats plus a small number of hens, pigs, goats and cattle brought in by settlers. There are masses of coconut groves, eucalyptus trees, cinnamon and vanilla bushes.

Counting different types of terns on African Banks in the Seychelles. These remote uninhabited islands provide the largest breeding grounds in the world for these migratory birds.

It is thought that the Seychelles were first discovered by Arabs travelling in dhows with lateen sails. Then in 1502, Vasco de Gama, the famous Portuguese explorer, landed on Mahe. In the eighteenth century, the British and French fought over the rights to colonise the islands and they changed hands several times. The Seychelles gained their independence from the British on 19 June 1976. Now the islands are an important breeding area for sea birds. It is thought that over 2½ million birds nest and breed there each year.

We stayed for nineteen days. Twice we climbed Trois Frères mountain (The Three Brothers) and Mount Siebert with Roger Wilson of the Botanical Gardens. We were trying to find, identify and map two species of plants: the *Toxocarpus* vine – only thirteen specimens of which have been discovered – and the jellyfish tree. This tree is extremely rare, and strange in that it produces mature seeds which do not appear to germinate. One way to identify the tree is from its fruit which looks just like jellyfish.

Eight of us moved to North Island which is about 7 square kilometres in size and only has twenty-five inhabitants. We spent three days searching for frogs, lizards and beetles. The rest of the YE's sailed in the *Eye of the Wind* to Frigate and Curieuse Islands to search for the *Toxocarpus* vine, giant land tortoises, magpies, robins, caecacians and geckos.

Later, we all returned to Port Victoria to carry out a marine survey of several of the neighbouring islands. This was for the St Anne Marine National Park which had just been formed to protect all marine life within the boundaries of the park. Trish Holdway took six of us at a time in the inflatable, while the others snorkelled the reefs. We saw sting-rays, octopi, moray eels, hundreds of varieties of fish, hard and soft coral and two types of waving sea grass.

Soon we moved on to the African Bank Islands. We had been asked to conduct a census of a nesting bird colony on North Island. There were sooty, crested and noddy terns, audobons, shearwaters, boobies, herons and frigate birds. It was the first time a large group of people had studied their behaviour and breeding patterns. But first we had to work out how to count them all. A briefing was held in the lower saloon of the ship. The plan was for one person to climb the 45-metre tower on the island with a camera and zoom lens, another to take photographs from the top of the ship's main-mast with a 500m lens, and for two YE's with cameras to be placed on the east and west side of the island.

Two lines of YE's trampled through the underbrush as the ship's horn blew and the tower flag was lowered. As the unfortunate birds took flight, the photographers snapped away for all they were worth. A computer would eventually count the birds from the blown-up photographs, but at a rough estimate there were around 30,000 birds on that sea breeding station.

We also caught sting rays with sharp-ended wooden spears, gathered tern eggs and made a study of the green turtle before we departed for East Africa.

We had been at sea for two months by the time we reached Mombasa, in Kenya. From the ship, Africa looked totally different from the Indian Ocean islands. It was much drier and, instead of palm trees along the coast line, we saw flat-topped acacia trees and a huge variety of wildlife.

We only had one month left, so we split into four groups to carry out several projects. I was in a group with four YE's from the ship and three Kenyan YE's who had joined us.

Our task was to help the Kenyan Rangeland Ecological Monitoring Unit (KREMU) to monitor wildlife movement in the Masai Mara Game Reserve in south-west Kenya. At KREMU headquarters in Nairobi, we met international wildlife biologists who told us about the animals' migration. Our job was to monitor a 50-kilometre strip of land from the base camp in the game reserve to north of the Serengeti Plains. We recorded the following pieces of information on data sheets: the numbers of males, females and juveniles in each herd; what kind of grass, bush or trees they were in; what they were doing; and which other species were with them. We used powerful binoculars to help us.

The annual migration from the north is one of the largest in Kenya. Thousands of milling wildebeest, gazelle, impala, giraffe, topi and zebra are on the move. These herds cross

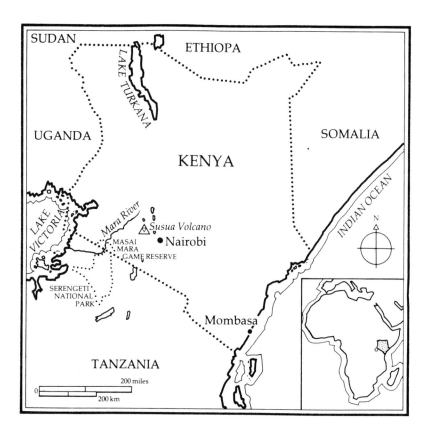

the Mara River and slowly eat their way south, always searching for the lushest, greenest grass that grows up after the rainy season. The animals spend four months in the Masai Mara each year before moving on into Tanzania and the Serengeti Plains. This cycle has been going on for thousands and thousands of years.

One night in particular comes to mind. Someone shone a high-powered torch into the bush and, as our eyes adjusted to the light, we saw hundreds of eyes reflected in its beam. A herd of 300 cape buffalo was moving to a watering hole. Lions roared continuously during the night, attracting females and fending off young males. Elephants lumbered through the tall grass around our campsite. It was a night to remember.

At dawn, we drove out of camp and crossed the Mara River where we saw vultures waiting for some unfortunate wildebeest to drown. There was an eerie silence. The vultures would occasionally swoop down to pick apart a floating carcass.

As we drove on, the scenery changed from the wide, flat plains of Africa's great Rift Valley to rocky escarpments

Zebras and wildebeest at a waterhole on the southern grasslands of Kenya in the Masai Mara Game reserve.

Young Masai spend much of their time tending their tribe's cattle and goats. Their staple diet consists of milk mixed with cow's blood.

where clumps of trees hid peering animals. Eventually we reached a Masai *manyatta* (village). The Masai people get up as dawn breaks, then wrap red ochre togas around themselves to keep out the early morning cold. The women light a fire with sticks and kindlewood that the young girls have gathered the day before. Young boys leave early to tend the herds of cattle, goats and shoats (half sheep, half goat) which are their only source of food and wealth.

When Masai youths enter manhood, at about sixteen years of age, they let their hair grow long. In order to symbolise a new life, everything they wear must be new. Red ochre is used to dye their togas and to paint their bodies from head to toe. Fathers give their warrior-sons new spears, while mothers and girlfriends make new beaded ornaments for them. Freedom and responsibility come with the new image. They can now marry and roam their Masai homeland at will. Their responsibility is to protect the herds of cattle from enemies, wild animals and famine. They are also responsible for slaughtering a cow for a special ceremony.

Masai men are very strong and the women and children within the tribe look up to the warriors for protection. Warriors feel a strong comradeship for each other and share everything, from women to food. Tradition demands that they never eat alone so, even today, warriors roam in groups to make sure that they will all get enough to eat.

Just as youths grow into warriors, so warriors become elders. We were fortunate enough to see an important ceremony called *eunoto*, meaning planting. The warden told me this only happens every four or five years when there are enough Masai warriors to be chosen to be junior elders. During the *eunoto* ceremony the elders of the tribe initiate the warriors into elderhood.

The ceremony began at about 3 p.m. Masai warriors, dressed in togas and bright necklaces of yellow, blue, red and white beads gathered in circles. They chanted songs. Two warriors advanced to the middle of the circle and, springing up on their feet, did several leaps about a metre off the ground. What an impressive sight! We were totally mesmerised by the noise, music and dancing. Then one of the women came up to me, took some ochre off her face with her fingers and smeared it on my forehead and cheeks. I became a Masai woman for the day.

A young Masai warrior, adorned with decorative necklaces and ear rings, has his face covered with orange ochre. He cannot wear these signs of manhood until he has been initiated as an adult warrior.

Later, the warden and I entered a hut where a group of young warriors were roasting meat. One of them cut off a slice of meat with his knife, gave it to me and indicated I should join the group. The warden was amazed. 'This is the first time I have ever seen a white woman invited to eat with the men,' he said. 'You are honoured.' For me, that day was the highlight of three months of non-stop excitement and interest. I could hardly believe it was happening.

But now it is all over. As I look back, I can't believe I will ever spend three months with better people. Our friendship had grown through storms at sea, struggles up mountains and explorations of deserted tropical islands. As we parted, I looked at their faces for the last time and realised that I would never forget them. How could I? We had shared so much together.

Diane Burroughes is now teaching environmental and conservation studies to 11–14 year olds in an overlander school, near Edmonton, Canada. In her spare time, she is an instructor on outward-bound-type courses in the Canadian Rockies.

PHASE 8a   June 1980 – August 1980

Camel Treks and Volcanic Craters

Charles Langat *Kenya* and Trevor Moss *England*

The undergrowth was so thick that it was impossible to see how far the summit really was. In the sweltering heat we climbed ridge after ridge thinking the next one would be the last. We had spent the whole of the previous day hacking away at the tangled foliage to travel only three-quarters of a kilometre. I could understand why no-one had ever climbed to the top of Mount Susua before.

But by 9 a.m. the vegetation began to thin out and we made faster progress. Then at 11 a.m., on 20 September, we reached the summit. It was a moment I will never forget. There was a tremendous feeling of achievement as we raised a pole with the Kenyan flag above and the white and blue Operation Drake flag proudly fluttering below. We had made it – the first successful ascent of Mount Susua.

Charles Langat, twenty-two years old, was one of twenty-two young Kenyans to participate in Operation Drake in Kenya. Although he had always enjoyed the outdoor life, he hadn't been able to join an exploration team until Operation Drake arrived in his home country.

Trevor Moss, also twenty-two, was equally interested in outdoor activities – he was a qualified pilot, marksman and holder of the gold Duke of Edinburgh's Award. Similarities in age, background, and love of the outdoor life made Charles and Trevor ideal companions to face one of the last unexplored areas of Kenya – the crater of Mount Susua.

But before they made their attempt on the summit, Charles was assigned to work on the Ark project, which involved constructing an 80-metre walkway bridge for the animals in one of the game reserves. Trevor was sent north to Lake Turkana to join a camel trek. Nine YE's, four herdsmen and fifteen camels were to travel 500 kilometres east of Lake Turkana – the fabled Sea of Jade – with Hussein, a biologist from the Natural History Museum in Nairobi.

We were walking with the camels, rather than riding them, because they were pack animals only and not trained to carry people. Also if we had wanted to ride, we would have needed thirty camels, not fifteen, and that would have been well beyond our budget. So, we had to walk.

Margaret Smart (England) leads a train of camels across the Koroli desert in north Kenya. Lack of drinking water, the intense heat and the thorny scrub made progress difficult and slow. The party followed in the footsteps of Count Teleki von Szek, the Austrian explorer, who discovered Lake Rudolph (now renamed Lake Turkana) in 1888.

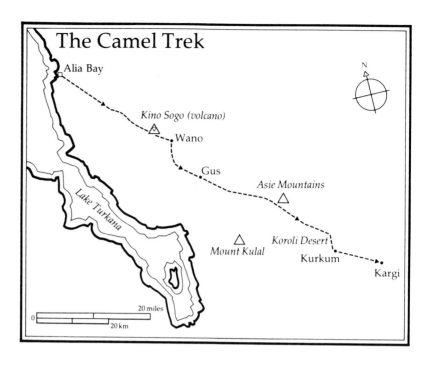

The Camel Trek

Our first day's trek only covered 16 kilometres. This was to break us in to the routine of starting at 7 a.m. – after a breakfast of sweet, salted tea and dried biscuit – and walking non-stop until we pitched camp at about 1 p.m. After that the heat became unbearable. Also, camels begin to show signs of exhaustion if they are made to walk for more than seven hours with a full load, and start to use up their reservoirs of water. They only need water every four days, as long as they are not pressed too hard, whereas we require a minimum of 6 litres in very hot weather.

Water was precious. As we could only carry a limited supply, washing was kept to an absolute minimum. At one point we didn't wash for five days and began to smell as bad as the camels. Whenever possible, we camped by waterholes so that we could replenish stocks and get some shelter under the thorny acacia trees which grew around the waterhole. But it wasn't possible to reach one of these oases every night and, on average, we had to camp in the desert two nights out of three.

One day we pitched camp under the Kino Sogo volcano which rises 500 metres above the desert plain. While we ate our lunch of porridge, dried biscuits and jam, and drank large mugfuls of tea, we learned from our camel herders that the volcano had never been climbed by white people. We decided to give it a go.

The climb was difficult, and not made any easier by the

extreme heat. The crags directly beneath the summit were sheer and we should really have used ropes. But after an exhausting and dangerous ascent, the view from the summit was fantastic, with the desert plains below stretching to Mount Kulal rising above the horizon in the distance.

When I was coming down, I met Richard Snailham and Phillip Todd on their way up. On their return to camp they told us of a rather interesting find they'd made. On the summit of Kino Sogo, there had been a small tin between some boulders. On the lid were the words 'Winchester Brand Cigarettes' and inside was a piece of paper. It was a note written in 1909 by the local District Commissioner, which said that he had climbed the mountain that year and anyone finding the tin should put their name on the paper. There were six people on the list, all Europeans, who had reached the summit between the years 1901 and 1951. It was annoying that those of us who were carrying pens missed the tin and those who discovered the tin had nothing to write with. Perhaps one of us will return some day to put the record straight and note that seven members of Operation Drake climbed the peak in 1980, seventy-one years after the first recorded ascent.

The next day we had a long walk through desert plains to the Wano waterhole. The average rainfall there is only 12 centimetres a year so there's very little vegetation, and in many places none at all. The scenery changed from hilly grasslands and plains, with the occasional thorny acacia tree, to dust bowls scattered with rocks from volcanos that had erupted millions of years before. The colour of the soil changed from white to yellow, to red, grey, green and even black depending on the minerals below the surface.

Between Wano and Gus the scenery changed dramatically. We were walking across sunbaked, rocky deserts. By 9 a.m. the heat was intense. Apart from Mount Kulal ahead of us, the landscape was flat and barren. During the first couple of hours, when people were fresh and alert, we would talk as we walked. But by late morning conversation dried and we plodded on as though sleep-walking. Thankfully, there was always a slight breeze in the morning that made the heat bearable and helped get rid of the smell of the camels. We quickly learned to walk on the windward side of the beasts, not only to lessen the stench but to avoid being sprayed by saliva and urine!

Each night we checked the campsite for scorpions with an ultra-violet lamp. A scorpion sting is agonising and at worst, can kill, although a two-day paralysis is more usual. Scorpions have a pigment in their skin which glows under ultra-violet light. Once we had seen one we caught it with a long pair of tweezers. The only really effective way of killing scorpions is to put them in a bottle full of cyanide poison. At one campsite fifty-eight were killed before we turned in. One had crawled into my rucksack and another appeared, glowing, on top of my campbed.

After we left Gus, waterholes became scarce and we had to cover a minimum of 33 kilometres a day. On the first day we ended up walking over 50 kilometres through the Asie range of mountains and then down into the Koroli desert. That night three of us used the same water for washing face, hands and feet. The rest was then used to heat our tins of food for the evening meal.

The next day it became essential to find water. Unfortunately, I awoke to find that my leg had become stiff after a nasty knock the day before so that bending my knee was very painful. But there was no option but to go on walking. Luckily, the exercise seemed to loosen the joint, although it was still very difficult to tackle a slope or start walking after a rest.

The day dragged on, but at last we reached the waterhole in the Balesa (dry river) Kulal. As we drew closer, however, we realised there were no animals or herdsmen nearby. When we looked into the well our worst fears were confirmed – it was dry. Our guides were amazed. They had never known it dry up before.

Trevor Moss sends a situation report to the expedition headquarters in Nairobi 600 km away on a Plessy 'Clansman' radio. This radio enabled the expedition to communicate directly with the main HQ in London from anywhere in the world.

We were now in trouble because the camels desperately needed water and we were down to survival rations. We had no choice but to march on to the next well at Kurkum, 11 kilometres away.

Again we had to walk through the heat of the afternoon but, this time, we were trying hard to conserve every drop of water. Our throats and mouths were as dry as sandpaper. We found Kurkum deserted.

At last we got there – but again we got a nasty shock when we looked into the first well and saw nothing but a puddle of yellowish water covered with birds' feathers. Fortunately we found another well, which had been sunk by UNICEF, a couple of hundred metres away. The water in this well was clear and cool. As an added bonus, there was a cattle trough which made an ideal bath.

The next day, Hussein and one of the YE's were being flown out to Nairobi, whilst the rest of us walked to Kargi, approximately 20 kilometres away. Together we celebrated the end of our 250 kilometre trek with a crate of beer which we managed to buy from the town's chief. Beer never tasted so good! We waved farewell to Hussein and Fiona at the airstrip then walked on to Kargi. There we waited for a land-rover to pick us up and take us to join Charles Langat and his party on the Susua crater project.

Mount Susua, situated some 70 kilometres due west of Nairobi, is the world's largest volcanic crater. The outer crater is 30 kilometres in circumference and the highest point, Ol Doinyo Onyoke, is 2,800 metres. Within the outer crater, there is just enough savanna grass to feed a few gazelle and some domestic Masai cattle. To get to the inner crater you have to cross a steep-sided 'moat', 250 metres deep. Because of this, many people believe that this is the last unexplored piece of territory in East Africa.

Although the summit of the inner crater appeared to be covered with thick bush, cacti and even cedar trees, we knew that water was going to be a problem. In the early morning light we could see steam issuing from vents in the side of the moat, but it was obvious that at best it would only make a very small amount of condensed water – possibly enough to support one person in an emergency, if it was free from sulphurous minerals – but certainly not enough to provide water for our large party. For this reason we spent a lot of time clearing an airstrip close to the base

Mt Susua remains the last major unexplored part of East Africa. Until the arrival of Operation Drake, few people had crossed the 250-metre-deep 'moat' around the central plateau. Scientists and Young Explorers had to be resupplied with water and food by parachute while they were surveying the plateau.

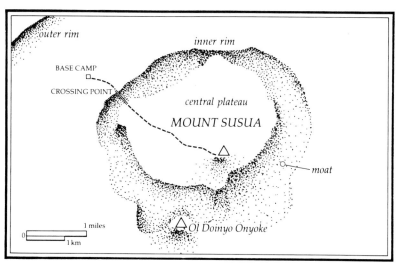

camp so that our small expedition aircraft – a British Army Air Corps Beaver – could parachute supplies of water to the small party.

The first thing we had to do was build a steel ropeway across the moat at its narrowest point. Unfortunately, this point proved to be where the moat's sides were at their steepest. It was also at the opposite side of the plateau to the summit, which rose gently for 4 kilometres through tangled vegetation.

Trevor and I were in the party which was to climb down into the gully and up the other side in order to blast a hole in the rock for the anchorage point. For this we had to take explosives strapped to our rucksacks, climbing ropes and a large supply of water. It was a terrible descent and climb. We had to cut our way through the foliage with machetes. Sweat trickled into my eyes and my rucksack, which carried 13 litres of water, got entangled with every branch and creeper.

When we had finally climbed the 250 metres to the lip of the inner plateau, John Blashford-Snell took the explosives and positioned the charges in a small crack in the rock. He came back and bellowed 'Take cover'. We all dived behind rocks and the blast sent boulders and stones flying in all directions. The boom of the explosion reverberated around the crater. It had done the trick and we were able to construct a secure anchorage point on our side of the moat.

Next day, I moved to the plateau with Liz Sutcliffe, Justin Bell and Trevor to try and find the easiest route to the plateau summit. We knew it was less than 4 kilometres away, yet we couldn't find an easy route. The barbs of the spear cacti, and a variety of thorns and spikes caught in our clothes and scratched our skin, while the flies rose in swarms, crawling all over our sweating bodies, into our eyes, ears and up our nostrils. The basalt rocks, divided by 15-metre-deep cracks, caused us the worst problems of all. We often had to crawl

The construction of a 300-metre steel wire ropeway across the 'moat' was an essential part of the resupply system. Water in jerrycans and equipment was ferried over and stockpiled before the Young Explorers made the assault on the summit of the central plateau.

Above *Charles Langat (Kenya) clambers up the side of the 250-metre-deep 'moat'. The Kenyan Wildlife Conservation Management Department are interested in developing the crater into a wilderness area for the more adventurous tourist.*

Opposite *Part of the survey party on the crater plateau. Trevor Moss is fourth from the left; Charles Langat stands next to the flagpole at the back.*

down into them to make progress. It was slow going; it took us several hours to travel no more than half a kilometre. The eventual assault on the summit was going to be no picnic.

Over the next few days we worked very hard indeed to get the ropeway in position and by 15 September the plateau party were settled into the forward base camp. I was put in charge of the ropeway and made responsible for getting equipment and stores across to the plateau party. The afternoon of the 15th saw the first load across. It was far more difficult than we had imagined. It took at least six people on each side to pull and steady the load.

By 17 September the plateau party were ready to leave forward base camp and make for the summit. The Masai tribe call the area 'The Lost World', making us think of discovering pre-historic monsters as we hacked our way through the creepy, sunless jungle. We didn't find any monsters of course, although Justin Bell came face to face with a leopard.

En route to join up with the plateau party we had scaled the moat and started to follow the path across the plateau. Nearby we could hear the barking of olive baboons, and it was not long before we came face to face with a group of

about forty of them, sitting on and around the track. At first the animals showed no fear – we were probably the first humans they had ever seen. They seemed inquisitive and our yelling and shouting did nothing to make them move off the path. But suddenly the animals obviously felt threatened and two large males rushed at us with teeth bared. Jim and I had machetes but the odds of getting away without being injured were slim. Luckily, the two animals stopped short and we retreated, hoping they would move along in their own time. After an hour or so, they did and we continued our journey. By mid-afternoon we had met up with the main group.

Progress was painfully slow, and it took a whole day to go three-quarters of a kilometre. The bush was so thick that it was impossible to know how far away the summit really was. Morale waned as we climbed ridge after ridge, thinking each time that the next one would be the last. The deadline to reach the summit was the next day, the 20th, but it was beginning to seem unlikely that we would get there on time. We returned to the spot where it had been decided to camp down for the night. The site was near to a clearing which was an ideal drop-site. At 5 p.m. the Beaver spotted the air identification panels and two 100-litre loads of water were dropped. Unfortunately, the food parcel containing chocolates and sweets came loose and we all watched with dismay as it spun off into the distance.

It felt good to be sleeping out in the open again that night – the temperature on the plateau was noticeably warmer than at base camp. The next day we made an early start and by 9 a.m. found that the bush was thinning. Even so, a lot of time was spent hacking down the vegetation in order that others could find our trail and that we would be able to retrace our route on the descent.

We reached the summit at 11 a.m. We were all exhausted but really proud of our achievement. When John Blashford-Snell arrived we had a flag-raising ceremony and celebrated with a beer apiece. It had taken our small party five days to cut the 3½ kilometre route to the summit. It took us only 3½ hours to return to base camp!

Charles Langat returned to Kenya to work in the Standard Bank of Nairobi. He is trying to form a Kenya branch of the Operation Drake Fellowship. Trevor Moss is an indemnity insurance broker in London. He was an instructor on the first Operation Drake Fellowship course in Scotland in July 1981.

PHASE 9   August 1980 – November 1980

Pyramids, Airships and the Atlas Mountains

Anne Wotton *England*

The wind increased to Force 8. The *Eye of the Wind* was almost surfing on the huge rollers. Our square sails strained white against a deep blue sky; as the wind whistled through the rigging the whole ship vibrated. Ahead, about thirty dolphins played around the bows, leaping over the white flecked rollers and twisting in the air, grinning – so it seemed – with delight. That day we achieved the ship's fastest run on the two-year voyage – 358 kilometres in 24 hours – and we had only been on board for three days! This was going to be some trip.

Anne Wotton had already travelled a great deal. As an army officer's daughter, she had been brought up in several European countries and had lived in Malaysia for two years. But she had never been to East Africa. When Capital Radio sponsored her to join Operation Drake, she was twenty-two years old and had just completed her training as a medical photographer at a dental hospital in London. She left London a few days after her final exam. It was not until the Eye of the Wind *reached the Red Sea, past the Horn of Africa, that Anne received her exam results over the ship's radio. She had good reason to celebrate: a speed record broken and an examination passed.*

In the Red Sea, the wind dropped and with it our speed. Without the cooling wind, the heat was unbearable. Even a swim didn't help – the sea was as hot as a bath. The heat grew worse and worse and sunburn became a real problem as temperatures soared above 50°C. Although we rubbed on lashings of sun lotion, lots of people still burned. We had to drink water almost continually to replace the liquid we lost by sweating and, at night, we had to sleep on deck as the heat below was intolerable. Heat was reflected off the metal decks; many YE's burned their feet on them and blistered their hands on the metal rails. As we had almost stopped moving because of the lack of wind, we had to start the engine. The fumes and noise made things even worse. Two and a half weeks after leaving Mombasa, we arrived at Port Sudan.

Port Sudan proved a new experience for us. The markets, where we bought more stores for the ship, were very smelly, dusty, crowded and squalid. In one of the restaurants, where several of us tried out the local dishes, scrawny cats climbed all over the tables and tried to join us in our meal. At the dockside, the crew of a British tanker handed over a racing pigeon which they had picked up exhausted in the Bay of Biscay and asked us to take it back to England. It made itself quite at home on the poop deck eating large amounts of split peas. It wasn't too popular, though, when it made white messes on our highly polished brasswork and scrubbed decks.

From Sudan, we moved north-west under engine power. Our skipper dropped anchor for a day alongside a coral reef called Sangareb. There we had our first taste of snorkelling, diving into the beautiful world that exists under the Red Sea – fabulous coral and multi-coloured fish, which I had only ever seen before in aquariums. Here they flitted and darted freely through the coral and seaweeds, dappled in sunlight. They were an exquisite sight.

As we continued north, the weather got progressively worse and we ended up having to seek shelter in Mersa Zeitza Bay, not far from Port Suez. Fortunately, our Egyptian co-ordinator organised an oil-rig supply vessel to take all but three YE's to Ismalia, in Egypt, where they were to plant trees and dig irrigation channels. The trees were being planted to stop the desert swamping the village with sand; the irrigation channels were needed to provide the 1,500 trees with water. It took twenty YE's five mornings, from 6 a.m. to 11 a.m., to complete the job.

Meanwhile, the *Eye of the Wind* set off north again for Port Suez. When we arrived, we were immediately surrounded by local traders in their small boats trying to sell leather camels, 'feelthy' postcards, brass plates and anything else they had on hand. They squabbled and struggled amongst themselves, standing in their unstable boats and stretching their wares towards us. Most wore dirty white robes and the traditional red fez on their heads.

By this time, the *Eye of the Wind* was in need of some repair. The relentless sun and sand storms had savaged the

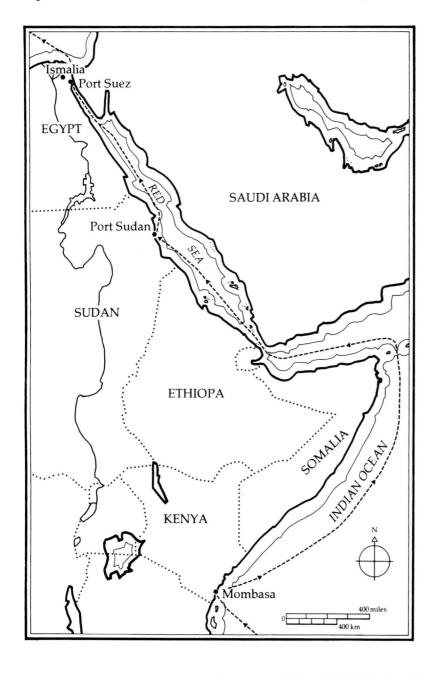

varnish work and the bare wood was quickly turning black as it soaked up salt water. It would soon become soft and rotten unless we did something about it. The constant battering of heavy seas had also stretched the rigging and this had to be re-tensioned. We three YE's, who were left on board, and the crew got to work to repair the damage.

At 4 a.m. we took aboard a pilot to help us navigate the Suez Canal. The canal is fairly narrow and we had to squeeze past huge tankers which were going in the opposite direction. We spent a lot of time waving at their crews, who looked down at us from a tremendous height. On one tanker we saw a bright red London bus. As it grew lighter we saw the desert stretching into the distance on both sides of the canal, strewn with abandoned blown-up vehicles, litter and derelict gun emplacements. Large packs of wild pi-dogs roamed the area and nosed around the debris. Eventually we reached Port Said where we moored between two huge tankers. Our masts and sails, dwarfed by the towering hulls of the modern ships, looked completely out of place. It was here, that our friendly racing pigeon left us for more comfortable quarters on a nearby tanker and the 'tree planters' returned, looking tanned, fit but rather dirty.

At last, we broke into the blue Mediterranean and headed for our next project in Italy. Temperatures dropped, although it was still warm enough to wear shorts and T-shirts. The sea was much calmer so we made good progress – so good in fact that we were able to spend a few days near Sicily, anchored alongside a small island called Lipari. There we were given the task of re-painting the *Eye of the Wind's* white hull. This was a pleasant job, made all the more enjoy-

The 41-metre-long Eye of the Wind *looks minute alongside the modern super tanker* British Resolution. *Surprisingly, this BP oiltanker has the same size crew as the* Eye of the Wind, *although it is 368 metres long and weighs 135,000 tonnes.*

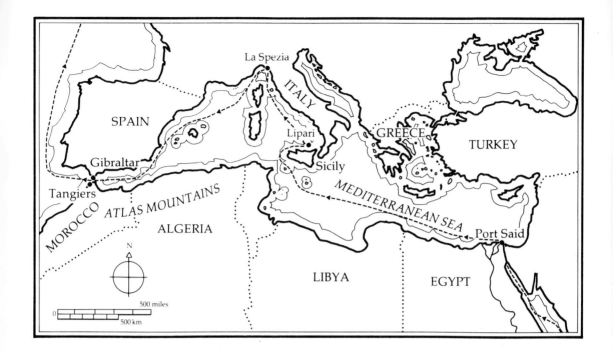

able by being able to slip ashore and buy something we had been dreaming about since we left Mombasa – ice cream!

Sparkling white, the *Eye of the Wind* headed for our next port of call, La Spezia in north Italy. Here, we were joined by two scientists. With the help of the YE's and the Goodyear airship *Europa*, they were to study pollution in the Gulf of Genoa. The Mediterranean had been chosen for this project because it covers one percent of the world's ocean surface, yet contains fifty percent of the world's most polluted seas.

The scientists were looking for more than just oil and chemical pollution. They were also trying to find traces of heavy metals, such as lead, mercury, zinc and cadmium. These metals are pumped into rivers as industrial discharge. Eventually, they are washed into the sea where they become concentrated in the bodies of tiny plankton. These animals are eaten by small fish, which are then eaten by bigger fish until finally, humans eat the large fish and become contaminated. As a result, people who rely on fish as a main part of their diet store dangerous levels of mercury in their bodies.

I was lucky enough to go up in the airship, or 'dirigible' as it is often called. We cruised slowly along the coast driven by two small propellers behind the cabin beneath the balloon. Then we saw her. What a magnificent sight! The *Eye of the Wind* was under full sail – brilliant white against the deep blue sea.

For two days, during daylight hours, we hovered above

The Eye of the Wind
teams up with the
airship Europa *off the*
north Italian coast to
conduct air and sea
pollution experiments.

the brigantine, one scientist in the *Europa* taking air samples, the other on the *Eye of the Wind* taking sea samples. With each sample they monitored the amount of mercury pollution. The Mediterranean certainly looked unhealthy from where I was. About 400 metres from the beach, the sea was a completely different colour from the rest. At the mouths of rivers, dirty sediment and effluent stretched far out to sea.

Once the experiments were complete, we said farewell to our friends on the airship and set sail for Gibraltar. They sent greetings to us from the air, a message which ran the whole length of the *Europa* on computerised lights: 'Greetings to Operation Drake . . . an expedition for young people from 27 nations'.

As the end of October drew near, it became colder and colder. We wore waterproof wet-weather gear for the first time and stayed below decks unless we had a particular job to do. Then very early one morning, as we came on deck, we saw the famous Rock of Gibraltar ahead of us.

Gibraltar (the only town on the rocky peninsular) was built after most of the older buildings had been destroyed by the Spanish in the Great Siege of 1779–83. The 'Rock' was acquired by Britain under the Treaty of Utrecht in 1713, after the war of the Spanish succession. It has remained British ever since and is a base for British naval ships. Tradition says that the day the island's hundreds of apes leave the rock, the British will leave the colony.

In Gibraltar we were joined by an experienced climber called Hamish Brown. He was to lead most of the YE's into the Atlas Mountains in Morocco where they would attempt to climb Jbel Toubkal, one of the highest peaks. Every morning we trained hard at an army barracks, because our walking muscles were weak after nearly three months at sea. Then we left for Tangiers on the hydrofoil. Finally, there was an eight-hour journey in a very crowded train to Marrakesh.

Our hotel was on the edge of the market with its teeming alleys and squares. Life must have changed little since the days of Drake. Metal and leather-workers, wood-carvers, kaftan-makers, jewellers, carpet traders all occupy separate areas. Frantic buying and selling, bargaining and arguing goes on all day. Towards evening, crowds gather on the main square around the story-tellers, quack doctors, snake charmers, Mauretanian dancers and sweetmeat sellers. It was all very noisy and colourful. We watched from the roof until dusk, when the sun set behind the minaret of the Koutoubia and the tomb of the city founder. A Moroccan meal ended a fabulous day.

In the morning a hired bus took our party into the mountains – 50 kilometres across the plains, up through forested foothills, and, finally, along a dirt track to the village of Imlil, where an alpine hut was used as a base. The first snows of winter had fallen on the peaks and the walnut leaves were sun-yellow. We could hear the singing of girls and men who were ploughing with mules in preparation for autumn sowing. It was an enchanting setting.

After the heat of the Mediterranean, it seemed strange to climb through the snow of the Atlas Mountains in Morocco. During the trek, five Young Explorers climbed Mount Toubkal, the highest peak in Africa north of Kenya.

At dawn the next morning, we walked in procession up the valley, past the casbah, round the edge of cultivated plain, and on to a shrine where the locals produced welcome mint tea. By the time we reached the small hut at 3,150 metres, it was snowing. It felt bitterly cold after the Red Sea. But, magically, it cleared in the night and at dawn the next day we set off again. The new snow, which drifted over the boulder fields and ravines, made for slow progress. Some of us only had stockings, instead of mits and plastic bags to wrap around our ankles to keep the snow out of our boots. Finally we made the Tizi-n-Ouagane on the main spine of the mountain range at 3,725 metres, higher than many famous peaks in the Alps. Beyond us lay a cloud sea stretching away into the distance to where the Sahara Desert began. The view was well worth the cold.

The next day, five of the group tried for Toubkal itself, while the rest of us returned to Imlil. It was another marvellous day. After dark one party went to a local village for *couscous*, Morocco's national dish. They returned to find that the five had indeed climbed Toubkal – the highest peak north of Kenya.

By the time we returned to the *Eye of the Wind*, the ship's rigging had been completely overhauled by master rigger

Wally Buchanan, who had flown from England especially for the job. The crew had also painted the metal and re-varnished all the wood.

And so, into the cold, raw Atlantic. It was good to be at sea again although the ship rolled and pitched as we laboured towards the Channel Islands through the Bay of Biscay. By the time we entered the English Channel, winds were gusting to Force 9 or more. I was wearing six layers of clothing in an attempt to keep warm. The ship was crashing and juddering as she ploughed into the huge waves. At times, YE's working on the jibs* in the bows would completely disappear underwater, then reappear soaking wet, only to crash down into the next frothing wave. It was a great relief to see the misty coastline of England appear above the racing waves.

Next morning, the sun came out as the storm clouds receded. All sails were set. In front of the crowd on Plymouth Hoe, we tacked* towards the entrance of the Barbican, the small harbour from which the *Mayflower* had departed for America in the sixteenth century. As we tied up alongside the Mayflower Steps after an absence of nearly two years we were met by the cheers of hundreds of well-wishers who had been waiting throughout the day to greet us. It was a proud moment to return to Plymouth 400 years after Francis Drake in the *Golden Hind*. We had sailed into a small niche in history.

We stayed for two days in Plymouth while friends and visitors clambered aboard for a look around the *Eye of the Wind* and to ask us innumerable questions. Onlookers stood for hours on the quayside staring at the beautiful lines of our brigantine. Admittedly, the *Eye of the Wind* did look magnificent. No doubt, they were imagining what it was like to experience the freedom of the sea and to be at the mercy of the elements far from land. Perhaps, too, they were thinking of those tropical islands and of the many kind and gentle people the *Eye of the Wind* had visited on her voyage around the world.

Anne Wotton stayed on board to help prepare the Eye of the Wind *for her next voyage to Australia. Just before the ship sailed from Southampton, she flew to Australia to make a 'walkabout', and to meet the many YE's who hope to be in Sydney for the ship's arrival in December 1982.*

Home is the Sailor

Linda Batt-Rawden
Producer, Capital Radio, London

Dawn broke as the *Eye of the Wind* turned slowly into the Thames estuary. She was on the last leg of her journey from Plymouth. As we motored with the tide, I stared at the dirty, brown, swirling waters and mused, 'It's now almost over. No more blue oceans, only grey skies and cold winds.' It started to drizzle. 'Yes,' I thought, 'We're home, really home.'

Linda Batt-Rawden was given the sort of opportunity you read about in fairy tales. She had been sponsored for a place on Phase 3 by Capital Radio in London. Just as she was coming to the end of that phase, a vacancy arose for a Capital Radio producer to accompany the expedition the whole way round the world. To cut a long story short, Linda got the job after a crash course on interviewing and editing. She was made responsible for sending a 5-minute programme back to London twice a week. These were broadcast every Wednesday and Sunday evening. Now her sixteen months with Operation Drake, during which she had travelled everywhere from the highlands of Papua New Guinea to the jungles of Sulawesi, were almost at an end.

At 4 p.m. we reached Greenwich and the imposing grey buildings of the Naval College on the banks of the Thames. We tied up in the shadow of the famous four-masted sailing ship *Cutty Sark*. We looked so small against this large black nineteenth-century tea-clipper. Yet the *Eye of the Wind* still looked elegant, beautifully white and sleek. The hard work in Gibraltar and Guernsey had been worthwhile. All we needed to do that afternoon was scrub the decks and bulwarks* and polish the brass. The brigantine would then be ready for her big day.

Later on I telephoned home. It seemed very strange to talk to my family after so long. They were coming up to London to see the arrival of the *Eye of the Wind* at Tower Bridge the next morning. I asked my sister to pick some holly and bring it with her so I could decorate the galley. After all, it was nearly Christmas. I also asked Mum if she had any geese on the farm – it would be so nice to eat a big, fat goose for Christmas dinner.

I thought back to last Christmas when we had been in Papua New Guinea. Between scrubbing and painting the cabins for the arrival of the Phase 6 YE's, I had iced the Christmas cake on deck in tropical temperatures. The trouble I had trying to get that icing to set before it all ran down the sides of the cake! This year, it would be very different. It was already freezing cold and I could see the ice beginning to form on the rigging.

That evening we had our last party on board. Everyone went a bit wild, although most of us went to bed reasonably early. I couldn't sleep. I was already nervous about our arrival next day and I tossed and turned in my bunk for ages. Suddenly, there was a noise on deck. It was half past one. Apparently some of the Americans had decided to go exploring and two policemen had caught them trying to climb the main mast of the *Cutty Sark*. Luckily they'd been stopped before they'd got too high. The rigging on that 112-year-old ship isn't very safe. Fortunately, the policemen let them off.

We were all up on deck at dawn, well before the pigeons. It was wet, cold and gusty. Worse still, the wind was blowing down river. It wasn't exactly sailing weather.

At 8 a.m. David Briggs, the Capital Radio producer who had been on Phases 1 and 2, came aboard. He was to send out a live broadcast about our arrival and he asked for my help. We checked that all the equipment was working well so David could broadcast from the crow's nest*. If anything went wrong I would take over from amidships, where I would be stationed with the reserve head-set and microphone. It all sounded very easy. But I had already bitten my nails to pieces with worry; it was worse than waiting for the dentist.

By 11 o'clock we were surrounded by a flotilla of small boats which were to accompany us up river. A beautiful Thames barge with reddish-brown sails also joined us. I listened in on the head-set. We were in contact with Capital Radio's outside broadcast unit at Tower Bridge. I heard Mike Smith say that there were thousands of people waiting to see us sail under Tower Bridge, alongside the Tower of London.

The atmosphere on board suddenly became tense. Captain Mike Kichenside emerged from aft* in full dress-uniform. He looked very smart. Colonel John Blashford-Snell, also in uniform, stepped aboard to join him. We took up our positions and waited for the word to cast-off. A sharp order from our skipper and the head rope was slipped. As the bows of the *Eye of the Wind* slowly started to turn amid-stream, the aft line was cast free. We were off. I took up my position amidships* and David Briggs slowly climbed the mast to the crow's nest to keep listeners in touch with our progress up the Thames.

There was a bustle of activity as the main staysail* and the inner and outer jibs were set. Bindings were taken off the three lower square sails, but Captain Kichenside, who had carefully been watching the direction and speed of the wind gusts, decided not to set them. As we rounded the first bend, the wind whipped across our beam causing the *Eye of the Wind* to heel over* violently. Anxiously, the skipper glanced over his shoulder to watch the Thames barge, and our flotilla of small craft struggle against the vicious gusts. Suddenly, there was a rending crack. The Thames barge's top mast had broken and the red sail had crashed onto her deck.

Luckily everyone on board appeared to be alright. The wind gusts got stronger and our skipper gave the order to set the main sail. David started his broadcast just as the great gaff* was hauled up the main mast.

'What's going on down there?' asked David Briggs, perched precariously in the crow's nest. I explained that even in good weather it takes about sixteen people to haul the gaff up the main mast. It was particularly hard this time because the wind was trying to tear the sail out of our control. The *Eye of the Wind* was now crashing through the brown water at a terrific speed, churning up great white-crested waves in front of her bow. Soon, we had left the crippled Thames barge far behind to limp along as best she could. Then, as we rounded the last bend in the river, we really ran into trouble. The wind was on the beam* again,

Linda Batt-Rawden interviews Sara Budibent (England) about her experiences on a five-day jungle acquaintance course in Papua New Guinea.

and because we were making such speed, it seemed inevitable that we would go aground. The sail had to be brought in, fast. Every moment, we came closer and closer to disaster.

I dropped the headphones and microphone, hoping that David wouldn't need me, and rushed to help the others furl the sail. As we dragged at the heavy canvas, I kept seeing newspaper headlines in front of my eyes: 'Eye of the Wind runs aground as she nears Tower Bridge'. A bit over-dramatic, I know, but I could just see the awful picture of the brigantine stuck on a mud bank like a beached whale, with thousands of people craning their necks to see her. Not a moment too soon, the sails were stowed and we were able to use the engine to drive us to safety, away from the bank. It was a close thing.

Now Tower Bridge was in sight and the sun was out. What a magnificent picture, as the great bridge slowly began to lift and part in the middle. All the YE's, in their dark blue sweaters scurried aloft to man the yards*. I was rather envious. I would have loved to drop my microphone and climb up there to see the great iron bridge open to greet us – and look at the people gathered there in their thousands. A sea of faces everywhere, along the embankment, by the bridge, in windows, on rooftops and in doorways. As we passed under the bridge, all the YE's waved to acknowledge the cheers from the crowds and the hoots from ships, tugs, barges and boats alongside the embankment. A Beaver and a

Hercules aircraft flew low overhead with a deafening roar. The *Eye of the Wind* had braved the mighty oceans of the world – like the *Golden Hind* 400 years before – and had returned home safely.

The brigantine turned slowly in mid-stream near the naval cruiser *HMS Belfast* and then returned under Tower Bridge to moor alongside St Katharine's Wharf. Here, the skipper waited for high tide to take the *Eye of the Wind* through the lock and finally into St Katharine's Dock itself where she would be berthed for the next two weeks.

Once the last warps had been made fast, I just felt numb. I wanted to run away and hide. After two years it was all over. But there were lots of people to see: family, friends, YE's, Operation Drake sponsors, organisers and schoolchildren whom I'd met just before I left. It was a bit like a family wedding, when you see people you haven't seen for ages and they say, 'How are you?' or 'Haven't you grown?', never anything sensible. It was terrible. Eventually I sneaked back to the *Eye of the Wind* and spent the rest of the afternoon in the galley serving cups of tea to visitors.

During the next week our evenings were filled with reunions. Operation Drake members came from all over the world to talk about old times and their plans for the future. They came from Iceland, Hongkong, Kenya, Panama, Australia, New Zealand, America, Canada . . . the list seemed endless. Why had they come? Simply because the friends they had made on Operation Drake were worth travelling half way round the world to meet again.

Our days were equally full. The *Eye of the Wind* attracted many visitors, and those of us living on board spent many hours proudly showing them around. By the end of the week, all of us were dead tired.

Then Friday came. This was our big day. Our Patron, HRH The Prince of Wales, was to visit the *Eye of the Wind*. The usual T-shirted and blue-jeaned YE's underwent a rapid transformation. Suits and dresses were the order of the day.

It's funny how nervous you can get meeting someone like Prince Charles. You know he's quite human, yet meeting someone who will one day be king is rather nerve-racking. I certainly felt scared. But he was very good at putting us all at ease and he had groups of YE's roaring with laughter.

Operation Drake hasn't changed my life – it has changed my attitude to it. I have seen for myself that many people will never own a colour television, an estate car or smart

His Royal Highness The Prince of Wales, the Patron of Operation Drake, talks to Neil Johnson (England), Amanda Roberts (Aus.), Tony Short (Aus.), Toby Roberts (England) and Margie Brookes (Aus.). In all, Prince Charles spoke to 214 Young Explorers from around the world, who had come to London to see the arrival of the Eye of the Wind.

clothes. Yet, possessions like these – nice as they are – are not the most important things in life. I now see the value of things I'd previously taken for granted – education, doctors, dentists and medical welfare. Just as important is having freedom of speech, the right to say 'the government is a load of rubbish' if I really want to. Perhaps, most important of all, I learned to be more tolerant and to respect different cultures, religions, ideas and ideals.

I also learned to endure. Many times I'd wanted to give in and go home to hot water, clean clothes, to a country where ticks or leeches don't drop from the trees into your hair and onto your skin and where you don't find poisonous snakes in the lavatory. There were times when I said, 'I can't do it' – but I did. Somehow, it got easier once you'd started. It would have looked a bit silly to sit down in the middle of the jungle and refuse to walk any further because I felt a bit tired, especially when a few more kilometres would get me to a tent, a camp fire, and safety!

Of course, knowing these things doesn't make finding a job any easier. But there is still room for people who are energetic and determined. For example, YE's are now making plans to explore remote areas in far-off countries, to help hard-pressed scientists collect insects or plants that are rapidly becoming extinct, or to help with community projects in underdeveloped parts of the world. It's not easy to make things happen, but you can – if you have the will.

Linda Batt-Rawden now runs 'Capital Venture', an advisory centre for young listeners to Capital Radio who wish to go on expeditions or work on community projects in Britain or overseas.

POSTSCRIPT

The Operation Drake Fellowship

Lieutenant–Colonel John Blashford–Snell MBE
Royal Engineers

When the *Eye of the Wind* returned to St Katharine's Dock in London after her two years' voyage around the world, over two hundred Young Explorers were waiting to greet her and to meet our Patron, Prince Charles. Their enthusiasm made us aware that there should be some sort of follow-up to Operation Drake which would encourage young people to take a positive lead in helping other youngsters in their own countries. We felt that the committees, which had been formed so patiently over the past three years in many different countries, should be kept going, even if they couldn't be as active as before. They had all done such sterling work and had often developed talents and abilities that had not been recognised before.

So it was that the Operation Drake Fellowship was born. Everybody involved believed that the first priority was to give boys and girls from the inner-city areas of London the chance to experience the fun of an expedition. With the help of many Young Explorers from Operation Drake, a programme of two-week courses in Scotland and Wales was arranged, and these have now been running continually since June 1981 for up to twenty young people at a time. Plans are also being drawn up for the first Operation Drake Fellowship project – the Black River Expedition in Honduras, Central America – where young people will help Carib and Mosquito Indians build a canal linking two villages, assist in the excavation of an eighteenth-century English fort on the coast and search for pre-Colombian archaeological sites in the jungle.

But this is just the start. A plan has been put forward by Mr Will Farish of Houston, Texas, to commemorate the founding of Virginia in America by another great Elizabethan explorer, Sir Walter Raleigh. Raleigh founded the colony in 1584 and as a direct result, introduced tobacco and potatoes to Europe.

It is intended that Operation Raleigh will be organised on the lines of Operation Drake and will start in 1984, 400 years after the colony of Virginia was founded. It will last four years and should involve over 4,000 young people aged between seventeen and twenty-four. There could be over forty nations participating in expeditions in fifteen countries, where major scientific and community projects will be carried out. The expedition will return to the USA and then to Britain in 1988. You can't get more ambitious than that, can you?

If you would like to join an expedition, perhaps the easiest way is to become a member of an adventure club or the scouts or guides at school, or an exploration society at university. It is also very advisable to go on an Outward Bound course which gives you an opportunity to discover your own strengths and weaknesses. The Duke of Edinburgh's Award scheme is another excellent way to gain experience.

Certainly, any experience you obtain in this way is a very useful qualification when you go before a selection board. You should study the reports of other expeditions and see how they were organised. It is also a good plan to read books about expeditions and outdoor skills. Then, if you are lucky, you may find yourself travelling to some remote part of the world on the adventure of a lifetime.

If you decide to plan your own expedition I strongly recommend that you try to select a project which will in some way, no matter how small, benefit mankind or help other people. A good motto is 'Service before self'. I wish you the very best of luck.

Glossary

Words in italics have separate entries in the Glossary.

Aft
Towards, near or at the stern (rear) of the boat or ship. 'Looking aft' is looking towards the stern.

Aloft
Overhead. To 'go aloft' is to climb the *rigging* up the mast and work on the sails.

Amidships
The centre part of a ship, or a command to the helmsman to turn the wheel until the rudder is in line with the *keel*.

Beam
The width of the ship or boat at its widest point.

Boom
The *stay* (or pole) which extends at right angles from the mast parallel to the deck, to which the bottom of the *sail* is attached.

Bow
The forward end of a ship or boat

Brigantine
A type of sailing ship so described because of its *rig*. It has two masts. The fore mast has four square *sails*. There are twelve other sails when all sails are *set*.

Bulwark
A parapet round the deck of a vessel which prevents things from falling overboard.

Buntline
A rope attached to the foot of a *sail* which passes over the *yard* and down to the deck. When it is pulled it raises the foot of the sail, so pulling the bunt (or bulk) of the sail up to the yard.

Cast-off
To let go any lines (often made of rope) which tie the ship or boat to another object.

Clew
The lower corners of a square *sail*.

Crow's nest
A small platform near the top of the *main mast* for a lookout to observe the horizon.

Deck house
Cabins or structures which are above the level of the deck. The *Eye of the Wind* has two deck houses, the aft and the for'ard. The aft deck house contains the laboratory and radio room, the for'ard deck house contains the *galley* and upper saloon.

Downhaul
A line which is pulled to lower a *sail* or *yard*.

Forecastle (Fo'csle)
The sleeping quarters closest to the *bow* of the ship or boat.

Fore (For'ard)
Forward. To 'Look for'ard' is to look towards the *bow* of the ship.

Fore and aft
Along the length of a ship or boat.

Foredeck
The area of deck in front of the fore mast.

Furl
To roll up the *sail* and secure it to the *yard* or *boom*.

Gaff
The pole to which the top of a four-sided *fore and aft sail* is set.

Galleon
A term generally used to describe the Spanish men-of-war (or large

Galley   sailing ships) in use during the time of the Armada (i.e. in the sixteenth century).

Galley   The kitchen or cooking area aboard a ship or boat.

Halyard   A rope, wire or chain by which a *sail*, flag or *yard* is *set*.

Heave-to   To slow or stop the boat by turning into the wind and letting the *sails* flap free. Only done for a short time.

Heel over   When a sailing ship or boat lies on its side from the force of the wind.

Hold   Cargo space below deck level.

Hove-to   See *Heave-to*.

Hull   The outside shell of the ship or boat.

Jackstay   A metal rail running along the top of the *yards*.

Jibs   The foremost triangular *sails*.

Keel   The fixed underwater part of a sailing ship or boat, used to prevent sideways drift and to provide stability.

Main mast   The largest mast; the centre mast in a three-masted vessel.

Man the yards   A command instructing people to go *aloft* and position themselves along the *yards*, either in preparation for *setting* or *furling* the square *sails* or, more usually, for ceremonial occasions when the entire crew links hands and stands on the yards.

Poop deck   The highest deck above the *quarterdeck*.

Quarterdeck   The upper deck towards the stern of the ship or boat.

Rig/rigging   The system of wires and ropes employed to keep the masts in place and work the sails.

Sail   A square or strip of canvas either hung from a *yard* or *stay* to catch the wind and so propel the sailing ship or boat forward.

Set sail   To set sail is to haul up the sails in preparation for the start of a voyage.

Sextant   A navigational instrument used for measuring the altitude of stars, planets and the sun to determine the position of a vessel.

Sheet   A line which is attached to the lower corner of a *sail*.

Spar   A stout pole.

Splicing   A method of joining ropes.

Square rig   A method of setting four-sided *sails* which hang down from the *yards*.

Stay   A long rope or wire supporting a mast.

Tack   To change direction by turning into the wind.

Top gallant   The third section of a mast above the topmast.

Watch   A division of the crew into teams to carry out a particular task between specific times.

Weigh anchor   To raise the anchor from the sea-bed.

Whipping   A method of preventing the end of a rope becoming unravelled.

Yard/yardarm   A *spar* crossed to the mast for the purpose of hanging the four-sided sail.